Introduction to AI
Theory and Applications

by Andrew Robbins

Level 5

IBC パブリッシング

はじめに

ラダーシリーズは、「はしご（ladder）」を使って一歩一歩上を目指すように、学習者の実力に合わせ、無理なくステップアップできるよう開発された英文リーダーのシリーズです。

リーディング力をつけるためには、繰り返したくさん読むこと、いわゆる「多読」がもっとも効果的な学習法であると言われています。多読では、「1. 速く 2. 訳さず英語のまま 3. なるべく辞書を使わず」に読むことが大切です。スピードを計るなど、速く読むよう心がけましょう（たとえばTOEIC® テストの音声スピードはおよそ1分間に150語です）。そして1語ずつ訳すのではなく、英語を英語のまま理解するくせをつけるようにします。こうして読み続けるうちに語感がついてきて、だんだんと英語が理解できるようになるのです。まずは、ラダーシリーズの中からあなたのレベルに合った本を選び、少しずつ英文に慣れ親しんでください。たくさんの本を手にとるうちに、英文書がすらすら読めるようになってくるはずです。

《本シリーズの特徴》

- 中学校レベルから中級者レベルまで5段階に分かれています。自分に合ったレベルからスタートしてください。
- クラシックから現代文学、ノンフィクション、ビジネスと幅広いジャンルを扱っています。あなたの興味に合わせてタイトルを選べます。
- 巻末のワードリストで、いつでもどこでも単語の意味を確認できます。レベル1、2では、文中の全ての単語が、レベル3以上は中学校レベル外の単語が掲載されています。
- カバーにヘッドホーンマークのついているタイトルは、オーディオ・サポートがあります。ウェブから購入／ダウンロードし、リスニング教材としても併用できます。

《使用語彙について》

レベル1：中学校で学習する単語約1000語

レベル2：レベル1の単語＋使用頻度の高い単語約300語

レベル3：レベル1の単語＋使用頻度の高い単語約600語

レベル4：レベル1の単語＋使用頻度の高い単語約1000語

レベル5：語彙制限なし

Contents

読み始める前に

私たちの身の回りでは、多くのAI (artificial intelligence) が活用されています。とはいえ、AIは著しい進化を遂げる一方で、多くの課題を抱えているのも現状です。本書では、そうしたより身近になったAIの定義、歴史、私たちの日常に今後どのような影響を与えるかなど、シンプルな英語でまとめています。将来、AIは私たちの生活、学校、ビジネスなど、あらゆる場面でさらに重要な役割を果たすことになるでしょう。

ここに本書に出てくる主な略語をまとめました。他のAI関連用語は巻末のワードリストに詳しく説明していますので、英語を読み進める上で参考にしてください。

ADAS advanced driver assist system
先進運転支援システム

AGI artificial general intelligence
汎用人工知能

AI artificial intelligence
人工知能

AIEQ AI Powered Equity ETF
AIEQ《AIが運用する上場投資信託》

ANI artificial narrow intelligence
特化型AI

ANN artificial neural network
人工ニューラルネットワーク

ASI artificial super intelligence
人工超知能

AVI automated video interview
自動ビデオ面接

CNN convolutional neural network
畳み込みニューラルネットワーク

ETF	exchange traded fund 上場投資信託
FNN	feed-forward neural network 順伝播型ニューラルネットワーク
GPT-3	Generative Pre-trained Transformer 3 GPT-3《文章生成言語モデル》
GUI	graphical user interface グラフィカルユーザーインタフェース
HFT	high-frequency trading 高頻度取引
KNN	k-nearest neighbors algorithm k近傍法
LaMDA	Language Model for Dialogue Applications 対話アプリケーション用の言語モデル
MAD	mutually assured destruction 相互確証破壊
ML	machine learning 機械学習
NLP	natural language processing 自然言語処理
NLU	natural language understanding 自然言語理解
RTS	real-time strategy リアルタイムストラテジー
SDQ	Smart Data Query SDQ《AIを用いたデータ出力要求》
SVM	support vector machine サポートベクターマシン
TSP	traveling salesman problem 巡回セールスマン問題
UBI	universal basic income 最低所得保障

Introduction

Artificial intelligence (AI) is everywhere. It's not a super-intelligent digital horror determined to destroy all humans—not yet, anyway. But it does affect all of us in our everyday lives, and its abilities and influence are increasing every year. In fact, AI is changing so rapidly that every draft of this book had to be revised according to new advances in the field.

So what is AI, exactly? Is it a tool to use, a weapon to fear, or perhaps even a friendly companion to chat with? You could argue that AI is all of these and more. You're likely aware of some of the places AI is used. If you've ever gotten a recommendation from an audio or video streaming service, you can thank AI for that. The same goes for products suggested by the e-commerce sites you use. But did you know that AI keeps spam out of your email inbox and helps you unlock your phone with your face? It prevents fraud in banks, it helps design new medicines, and it's even being used by some police forces to help solve crimes.

This might surprise you, but I didn't complete

the last sentence by myself. I used an AI writing program to suggest what should come after "design new medicines." The program also suggested that it's used to "help soldiers on the battlefield" and "teach children"—both true. When it comes to writing assistance, AI isn't just a simple grammar checker anymore. It is transforming entire industries from journalism to advertising to showbiz.

But where are the killer robots? Movie franchises like *The Terminator* and *The Matrix* warn us of a digital uprising. Meanwhile, the *Star Wars* and *Star Trek* universes suggest that humans and AI could be working together to accomplish the same goals. Those sorts of AI, called Artificial General Intelligences (AGIs), are still science fiction. AI has yet to achieve consciousness or even general human-like abilities. AI may beat our best chess players with ease, but those same programs can no more carry on a conversation than a toaster can (even AI-powered toasters—yes, they really exist). AI programs are mostly built to accomplish fairly simple goals. They are incapable of being used to complete unrelated tasks, and often related ones, too (one major exception is GPT-3, discussed later in the book).

The field of AI is vast. To reveal all of its many hidden layers (that's an AI joke—you'll see why soon) would require thousands of pages and an advanced degree or two. Therefore, the purpose of this book is to provide a basic introduction to both technical concepts and applications of AI. You'll learn how AI has shaped our past and continues to shape both our present and our future. You'll also be given a chance to dive deeply into some topics to understand both the breadth and depth of the field.

While the definition of AI has evolved throughout the years, as you read this book—and consider AI in any other context—you're encouraged to think of AI as the study of intelligent agents. Intelligent agents are anything that tries to accomplish certain goals by taking autonomous actions based on how it perceives the world around it. We say that an agent is intelligent if its actions are rational. For example, the spell checker in your favorite word processing program can "see" (its perception) the text you're writing and "tell" (its action) you where it thinks you've made an error in order to fix as many spelling problems as possible (its goal). You can judge how intelligent the spell checker is based on how accurate you think its suggestions are and how many errors it detected (its rationality). Take some time to think about the AI around you and how their attempts to achieve their goals could be perceived as intelligent.

When it comes to understanding technical topics, some readers prefer to get a firm understanding of theory before looking at applications, while others prefer the other way around. In this book, you will find more discussions of theory in the "Foundations" section and more discussions of applications in the "Society" section. Feel free to explore the chapters in any order you please.

Foundations

Definition

What is AI? It's not the same as automation, although the two terms are closely related. Indeed, AI is a type of automation. But automation has only two criteria: the use of some type of machine and a self-governing system. In the early 1800s, a French weaver named Joseph Marie Jacquard developed a Jacquard loom, which is a special type of loom used to weave complex patterns into fabrics. The loom made use of punch cards, which are cards punched with holes in them. The arrangement of the holes determined how the cords of fabric would be woven.

The Jacquard loom was certainly automated, but was it "intelligent"? When automation acts intelligently, we tend to consider it AI. But what is "intelligent"? It depends on the context. What we consider intelligent changes over time as we get used to machines achieving more and more complex goals. This brings about an interesting problem because the goalpost is always moving.

This problem is known as the "AI Effect," which can be summarized with Tesler's theorem: "Intelligence is whatever machines haven't done yet."

The invention of the Jacquard loom was revolutionary. Surely the people of the time considered using punch cards to produce textile patterns "intelligent." And punch cards were used to program computers all the way through the late 1970s. But today, people would not likely consider the Jacquard loom "intelligent." In two centuries, the goalpost has moved a long way.

The English Oxford Living Dictionary describes AI as "the theory and development of computer systems able to perform tasks normally requiring human intelligence, such as visual perception, speech recognition, decision-making, and translation between languages." The late Stanford Professor John McCarthy said that it was more generally "the science and engineering of making intelligent machines, especially intelligent computer programs."[1] McCarthy, who came up with the term, is recognized by many to be the father—or at least one of the fathers—of artificial intelligence. Stuart Russell and Peter Norvig laid the foundation for the modern approach of

AI, whereby intelligence is determined by the rationality of an agent's actions in relation to its goals. In this case, AI is considered the intelligence of those agents.

History

The idea of "intelligent machines" is an ancient one. Greek Mythology tells of Talos, a bronze giant constructed by Hephaestus, the god of fire, to protect the island of Crete. Every day, Talos walked around the island throwing very large rocks at enemy ships. Ancient Jewish folklore mentions a golem, a creature made from clay and brought to life with a type of magic. An expert of the Jewish religion wrote in the mid-17th century that he had even heard of a person who made a golem, and "it performed hard work for him for a long period."[2]

With the birth of the science fiction genre came works that planted the idea of AI firmly in people's consciousness, although the term itself had yet to be coined. Before the invention of the moving picture, there was perhaps no artificially intelligent character more well-known than Frankenstein's monster from Mary Shelley's *Frankenstein*, published in 1818. In the novel, a young scientist uses technology to give life to a creature he pieces together with old body parts. (Sadly, the monster kills a number of people, and the novel ends in tragedy.)

Meanwhile, various 17th-century philosophers were concerned with the idea that all rational thought could be made using a system similar to mathematics. Gottfried Wilhelm Leibniz, a German mathematician and philosopher, imagined a universal language of reasoning so precise that all arguments could be solved with calculation.

Coming into the 20th century, the speed of innovation became more rapid in both arts and technology. Karel Čapek, a Czech playwright, coined the term "robot" in his 1921 science fiction play *Rossum's Universal Robots*. The story is about a factory that makes artificial people created from synthetic organic matter. At first, the robots are happy to serve their human masters, but later they revolt and destroy the human race. The play gained international attention and premiered on

Broadway in 1922. The famous science fiction author Isaac Asimov, author of the *Robot* series of books, remarked, "Capek's play is, in my own opinion, a terribly bad one, but it is immortal for that one word. It contributed the word 'robot' not only to English, but through English, to all the languages in which science fiction is now written."[3]

Also toward the beginning of the 20th century, probability theory and other key AI concepts were further developed. On January 23, 1913, Russian mathematician Andrey Markov addressed the Imperial Academy of Sciences in St. Petersburg to discuss what are today known as "Markov chains." A Markov chain describes "a sequence of possible events in which the probability of each event depends only on the state attained in the previous event."[4]

A simple example is the internationally best-selling board game *The Game of Life*, known in Japanese as *Jinsei Gēmu*. In the game, there is a wheel with the numbers 1 through 10 on it. On every turn, a player must spin the wheel to determine how far their playing piece advances. Where they land depends not only on the spin of the wheel but also on the current location of their piece. The probability of landing on a specific space depends only on the location of the player's piece when spinning the wheel, not on how the piece landed on its previous space. Mapping out the probability to move from every location on the board to every other location forms a Markov chain.

A more everyday example is the predictive text feature on your phone. As you type, your phone can predict what word you are attempting to input, helping you save time. If you type "el," it might suggest "element," "elevator," or "electric," common words beginning with "el." (It might also suggest "Ellen" if it's learned that you often contact your friend Ellen.) If, however, you type "elep," it will likely suggest "elephant," rather than "elephantine" or "elephantitis," being that "elephant" is more probable.

Markov made his discovery by means of analyzing a work of poetry. By examining the order and frequency of consonants and vowels in Alexander Pushkin's *Eugene Onegin*, often studied by Russian schoolchildren, he concluded that Russian vowels and consonants tend to alternate. (English, in comparison, is rather consonant-heavy.) To most Russians, this may not have come as much of a surprise, but the means by which Markov came to his conclusion was groundbreaking.

In 1943, neurophysiologist Warren McCulloch and mathematician Walter Pitts proposed a model of artificial neurons, also referred to as "nodes," making a simple artificial neural network (ANN) using electric circuits. The concept of this model was further developed by Canadian psychologist Donald Hebb, who came up with a rule for updating the connection strength, or weight, between neurons.

ANNs, more commonly referred to as neural networks, draw inspiration from animal brains. In such brains, signals are sent between each neuron using connections called axions. ANNs can be "trained," which is why they are classified as machine learning (ML) models. ML is the branch of computer science that studies systems that can improve their performance when they're presented with new data. ANNs are usually not considered intelligent agents, but intelligent agents often make use of ANNs to accomplish their goals. In addition, ANNs are not structural copies of animal brains. Even today, scientists have yet to completely solve all the mysteries of the brain, let alone neurons themselves, so making a digital copy of a brain would currently be impossible. As recently as 2022, scientists discovered a new pathway for neurons to send signals to one another through cilia, the tiny hairs on their surface.

ANNs are organized into layers of nodes, and every ANN is made up of three types of them: input layers, hidden layers, and output layers. The nodes in input layers accept the initial input data. Hidden layers perform computations on the data based on the values of inputs and weights, and then determine how to pass along that data based on an activation function, which is a type of calculation. Output layers produce the results. What makes ANNs powerful lies in how the hidden layers are structured and connected.

In 1950, English mathematician and computer scientist Alan Turing published *Computing Machinery and Intelligence*, which explores the idea of whether machines can think. In the book, he proposes a test, which he calls an "imitation game," to determine whether a machine can demonstrate intelligence. The test involves three participants: two humans and a machine. All participants are in separate locations, so they cannot see or hear each other. One human and the machine have a text-based conversation. The other human is an evaluator, who can see only the text of the conversation. The evaluator must try to determine which participant is the human and which is the machine. If the evaluator cannot reliably tell them apart, the machine is said to have passed the test. Now known as the Turing test, this test has had a profound impact on the field of AI.

A number of algorithms important for the development of AI started appearing around the time Turing came up with his test. An algorithm is a set of concrete instructions that are used to solve a particular problem or complete a specific task. For example, an algorithm could organize a list of names alphabetically. Algorithms are not just processes performed by machines. Even a recipe for baking a cake is an algorithm as it includes a set of clear steps to complete the task.

Perhaps the first recognized computer algorithm was developed by English mathematician Ada Lovelace in the early 1800s. Curiously, while Lovelace, like the Jacquard loom, appeared well before the invention of digital computers, she's still considered the first computer programmer. In her notes that describe how a computer might be programmed, she described a simple loop. In programming, a loop is a set of instructions that repeat until a certain condition has been met. The apps on your smartphone make use of thousands of loops every single day.

Another important algorithm was proposed in 1951 by Evelyn Fix and Joseph Hodges, both statisticians who taught at the University of California, Berkeley. The k-nearest neighbors algorithm (KNN) is one of the simplest machine learning algorithms, as well as perhaps one of the most frequently used. KNN can be described as both "supervised" and "lazy." This doesn't mean that it has a boss screaming at it to get back to work every few minutes; "supervised" and "lazy" are a way of classifying ML algorithms.

ML algorithms largely make use of one of two types of techniques: supervised learning or unsupervised learning (note that there are also semi-supervised and self-supervised learning techniques). Supervised learning algorithms train, or "supervise," models using labeled data to classify it or make predictions. Labeled data is data that has a tag, such as a type or a number. Supervised learning algorithms are used for two different kinds of models: classification and regression.

Classification models do exactly what you expect: they classify data into categories. They can classify emails, sending them into separate folders for promotions or spam; they can classify images, helping self-driving vehicles determine the difference between obstacles like bicycles and people; and they can even classify both digital and real-world viruses based on their different features.

Unlike classification models, regression models do not output discrete values. Instead, they output a continuous quantity that shows the relationship between dependent and independent variables. Regression models can be used to predict such things as sales revenue, real estate market trends, and even the weather.

The main difference between supervised learning and unsupervised learning is that unsupervised learning does not use labeled data. This type of ML is useful for discovering patterns in data and is used for three main tasks: clustering, association, and dimensionality reduction. Clustering, perhaps the most widely used unsupervised learning method, groups data based on similarities or differences (e.g., a credit card company could spot fraudulent transactions). Association is a method for finding relationships between variables in large datasets (e.g., an e-commerce site might suggest buying sugar to someone who buys a 10 kg bag of flour). Dimensionality reduction reduces the number of dimensions in a dataset. This is often used to pre-process data before applying a supervised learning algorithm.

As for KNN being lazy, ML algorithms can be classified according to when they abstract from the data. If data is classified after the model receives the data, it is considered "lazy." In this case, it takes more time to classify the data. If data is classified before the model receives the data, it is considered "eager." In this case, it takes less time to classify the data, but there is an upfront cost of training time.

So given all of this, how does the lazy and supervised KNN work? It follows three straightforward rules:

1. Compute a distance value between the item to be classified and every item in the training dataset.

2. Pick the k closest data points (the items with the k lowest distances), whereby k is the number of neighbors "voting."
3. Conduct a "majority vote" among those data points. Then the classification that gets the most votes in the group is decided as the final classification.[5]

What's thought to be the first AI computer program came about in 1956. Computer scientists Allen Newell and Clifford Shaw, along with political scientist Herbert A. Simon created "Logic Theorist" (LT) to show that a machine could prove mathematical theorems. They were able to prove 38 theorems found in *Principia Mathematica*, which is a widely regarded work on the foundations of mathematics, written at the beginning of the 20th century.

The first version of their program, despite being recognized as AI, was not executed by a machine; it was executed by humans. All of the steps of the process were written on 3x5 index cards. According to Simon, "We assembled my wife and three children together with some graduate students. To each member of the group, we gave one of the cards so that each person became, in effect, a component of the LT computer program—a subroutine that performed some special function, or a component of its memory. It was the task of each participant to execute his or her subroutine, or to provide the contents of his or her memory, whenever called by the routine at the next level above that was then in control.

"So we were able to simulate the behavior of LT with a computer constructed of human components. Here was nature imitating art imitating nature. The actors were no more responsible for what they were doing than the slave boy in Plato's *Meno*, but they were successful in proving the theorems given them." Later, the team was able to run the program successfully on an actual computer.[6]

LT was one of the first "symbolic AI" programs. Symbolic AI, also known as "classical AI," "rule-based AI," and "good old-fashioned AI," is the branch of AI that involves representing human knowledge as facts and rules in computer programs (modern symbolic AI also includes ontologies). Symbolic AI dominated the field from the mid-1950s until the mid-1990s. During that time, many people believed they would be able to create a machine with human-like abilities using such methods.[7]

It's important to note here that there are different ways of classifying AI as well as different architectures of AI. The two main architectures are "symbolic" and "connectionist." Unlike symbolic AI, connectionist AI (discussed later in the chapter) attempts to model intellectual abilities using ANNs that grow more intelligent as they learn patterns and relationships in data.

There are also three categories of AI that generally describe their abilities: artificial narrow intelligence (ANI), artificial general intelligence (AGI), and artificial super intelligence (ASI). ANI, also referred to as "weak AI" or "narrow AI," describes all currently known applications of AI: they are all good at very specific or closely related tasks, like facial recognition or product recommendation. AGI, also referred to as "strong AI" or "deep AI" (not to be confused with "deep learning") describes AI that can understand or learn intellectual tasks much like a human, even when faced with unfamiliar situations. While AGI has yet to be achieved, you can easily recognize

AGI characters in science fiction, such as C-3PO in *Star Wars* and Agent Smith in *The Matrix*. ASI describes an AI that doesn't simply copy human intelligence; it surpasses it, able to perform tasks that are impossible for humans. It is assumed that ASI would be self-aware.

If ASI appears, the technological growth that would follow would be both radical and uncontrollable, resulting in irreversible and unforeseeable changes to the world. The point at which this occurs is what is known as the "technological singularity" or an "intelligence explosion." And with the arrival of AGI, ASI would probably be right around the corner because AGI would likely be able to evolve by itself without any help. But to develop AGI may require a new set of advanced algorithms and possibly more computing power than what is presently available.

These ideas were likely addressed in some manner in 1956 at the Dartmouth Summer Research Project on Artificial Intelligence (DSRPAI), hosted at Dartmouth College. John McCarthy and Marvin Minsky, co-founder of MIT's AI laboratory, gathered top researchers from a variety of fields to have an open-ended discussion about AI. Although the conference was neither as organized nor as widely attended as McCarthy had hoped, it was clear that most attendees agreed that AI was achievable. This conference is considered by many to represent the true birth of AI. There the term "artificial intelligence" was invented and AI was established as an academic field of research.

In 1958, *The New York Times* reported on an unbelievable invention. "NEW NAVY DEVICE LEARNS BY DOING: Psychologist Shows Embryo of Computer Designed to Read and Grow Wiser," the headline read. The article continued: "The Navy revealed the embryo of an electronic computer today that it expects will be able to walk, talk, see, write, reproduce itself and be conscious of its existence."[8]

Research psychologist Frank Rosenblatt had designed the Perceptron, which learned to understand the difference between cards marked on the left and cards marked on the right. This was the very first ANN. The following year, an ANN was applied to a real-world problem for the first time. MADALINE, short for Multiple ADAptive LINear Elements, was made to remove echoes on phone lines.[9]

MADALINE was a feed-forward neural network (FNN), which is the simplest type of ANN. The network contains no loops as none of the nodes connect back to previous nodes—information thus goes only in one direction: forward. FNNs are generally used for classifying binary patterns. MADALINE was made up of memistors. The term is a combination of the word "memory" and "resistor" because memistors are resistors with the ability to store information while also performing logic operations.

In 1963, economist James Morgan and sociologist John Sonquist developed the first regression tree algorithm. A regression tree is a type of decision tree, which is a supervised learning tool for classification and prediction. Decision trees are structured like a tree. They have a root node, which is the base of the tree, and they split into sub-nodes. When a sub-node connects to no further branches, it is called a leaf node, and it represents a possible outcome of the decision tree.

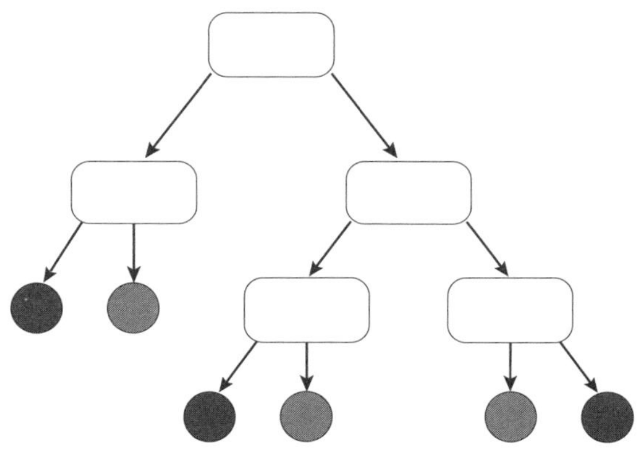

Decision tree[10]

Decision trees are not just used in computer science; they can be used as flowcharts to determine the optimal course of action in any given situation. For example, say you're trying to decide whether to have a picnic with your friends at the park, and you want to base your plans on the weather. The forecast could be your root node. If it's rainy (sub-node), you won't go. If it's overcast (sub-node), you might make a decision based on further sub-nodes that describe how cold or windy it might be. If it's sunny (sub-node), you might make a decision based on further sub-nodes for heat and humidity.

Decision trees are fairly easy to use and easy to understand, but they have a number of weaknesses that make them a poor fit for a variety of applications. In some cases, they frequently make errors. They can also take a lot of time to train. Further, changes to the data can require major structural changes to a tree.

ELIZA made use of decision trees and helped convince government organizations in the 1960s to invest in AI research. ELIZA wasn't a person, however. It was the first chatbot, created by Joseph Weizenbaum, an MIT professor and a major contributor to the field of AI. ELIZA performed natural language processing (NLP) using SLIP, a language invented by Weizenbaum. It then used pattern matching and substitution along with a prewritten script to produce replies as if it were a human.

Weizenbaum's script was based on the style of Carl Rogers, a famous psychologist who frequently used open-ended questions and rephrased things that patients said. Here's an example of a typical conversation with ELIZA:

Woman: Men are all alike.
ELIZA : In what way?
Woman: They're always bugging us about something or other.
ELIZA : Can you think of a specific example?
Woman: Well, my boyfriend made me come here.
ELIZA : Your boyfriend made you come here?
Woman: He says, I'm depressed much of the time.
ELIZA : I'm sorry to hear that you're depressed.
Woman: It's true, I am unhappy.
ELIZA : Do you think coming here will help you not to be unhappy?[11]

While many people agree that ELIZA did not pass the Turing test, the program still managed to make some people believe that they were talking with a human. And many were charmed by it. This was shocking to Weizenbaum, who intended for the program to "demonstrate that the communication between man and machine was superficial." He wrote of ELIZA, "What I had not realized is that extremely short exposures to a relatively simple computer program could induce powerful, delusional thinking in quite normal people." When an acquaintance at Stanford started promoting the idea that chatbots had actual therapeutic use, Weizenbaum strongly objected. But it was too late—chatbots were beyond Weizenbaum's control. Not only did other people start to develop chatbots, some of which were more advanced, but eventually, ELIZA itself even appeared in movies and video games as well.[12]

One of the results of Weizenbaum's invention was the naming of "the ELIZA effect." The Eliza effect is the tendency for people to assume that computer behaviors are comparable to human behaviors. For example, when a virtual personal assistant, such as Siri, says "sorry" when it can't perform some function, some people might feel that Siri is truly sad because of its inability to fulfill a request. In reality, Siri is simply an AI that has no feelings.

Another algorithm important to the development of AI was introduced in 1967. The nearest neighbor algorithm provided an approximate solution to the "traveling salesman problem" (TSP), which is studied by computer science students all over the world. The optimization problem can be stated simply: "Given a collection of cities connected by highways, what is the shortest route that visits every city and returns to the starting place?"[13] While TSP may at first seem useful only for travel agents and people who go on long road trips, the basic concept has applications ranging from DNA sequencing to microchip manufacturing.

The nearest neighbor algorithm can be summed up in five simple steps, given a graph of all of the vertices (cities, in the case of TSP):

1 Initialize all vertices as unvisited.
2 Select an arbitrary vertex, set it as the current vertex **u**. Mark **u** as visited.
3 Find out the shortest edge, or connection, between the current vertex **u** and an unvisited vertex **v**.
4 Set **v** as the current vertex **u**. Mark **v** as visited.
5 If all the vertices in the domain are visited, then terminate. Else, go to step 3.[14]

The nearest neighbor algorithm is not the optimal solution to TSP. In fact, a new, faster approximation was discovered as recently as 2020.

And the nearest neighbor algorithm can miss the shortest possible tour of the cities. Sometimes, it doesn't find a tour at all, even when one exists. But despite its shortcomings, it runs quickly, which makes it very useful.

Another widely used algorithm introduced in the 1960s was backpropagation. It was developed by several researchers, although its modern form was made in 1970 by Finnish mathematician Seppo Linnainmaa. The algorithm is used in supervised ML to train and improve an AI's performance. Essentially, you take the output of an ANN and compare it to the result you want in order to calculate an error value. That error value is then passed backward through the layers in the network to update the weights of the connections to make for a better output.

After a period of steady advances in AI, development slowed down significantly. AI developers were frustrated because many had underestimated the difficulty of building AI systems. They also lacked the computing power needed to make great progress. Funding and interest declined. The world entered what's known as the first "AI winter," which lasted from 1974 to

1980. But researchers didn't all give up on AI.

In 1979, Japanese computer scientist Kunihiko Fukushima published a paper that described a "neocognitron," a hierarchical, multilayered ANN. The neocognitron formed the foundation of convolutional neural networks (CNNs). CNNs enable ANNs to preserve required attributes that would otherwise be lost. Take an image, for example. An image is made up of pixels, each of which is a single dot with values that define its color and tone. However, each pixel is also situated in a certain position, and the proximal relationships between pixels get lost in a regular ANN. In a CNN, a hidden convolutional layer helps to prevent such relationships from being lost. That's why CNNs are used most frequently in such things as image classification and facial recognition.

The end of the first AI winter brought with it a new dominant approach to AI: expert systems. Expert systems are designed to answer questions about specific areas of knowledge as if they were actual human experts. They make use of facts provided by human experts as well as algorithms that apply rules to those facts in order to try to figure out new facts. Although the first expert systems were developed in the 1960s and 1970s, in the 1980s they helped produce a billion-dollar industry as corporations began to view them as absolutely necessary. XCON, an expert system developed at Carnegie Mellon University (CMU), helped the Digital Equipment Corporation (DEC) select computer parts to satisfy customer requirements. It saved the company tens of millions of dollars a year.

While symbolic AI led the way up until the first AI winter, researchers focused more on connectionist AI after it ended. In 1982, John Hopfield wrote a paper describing the Hopfield network, one of the first recurrent neural networks (RNNs). RNNs were further developed by psychologist David Rumehlart, who in 1986 published a paper on backpropagation in ANNs. In FNNs, data moves forward from one node to another, but in RNNs, a node's output can loop back as input to previous nodes. This structure gives RNNs a form of internal memory called content-addressable memory, which helps them remember things about their input. That's why they are well-suited for using sequential data such as text, speech, audio, and video to make predictions.

Funding for AI dried up again, and a second AI winter occurred from around 1987 to 1993. But research never completely stopped. In 1989, British computer scientist Chris Watkins wrote his Ph.D. thesis entitled "Learning from Delayed Rewards," which described Q-learning, an important reinforcement learning algorithm. Reinforcement learning is similar to supervised learning except that the model isn't trained using sample data; instead, it trains itself using trial and error. In other words, it learns from experience. You can see reinforcement learning in action on YouTube and other streaming services, as many developers have uploaded videos of video games learning to play themselves. Aside from gaming, reinforcement learning has a variety of applications, from NLP to autonomous driving.

While expert systems were a big deal in the 80s, in the 90s the field put its support behind a new idea: intelligent agents. The term "agent" broadly describes anything that can perceive its environment and take actions to accomplish its goals. Humans are agents, as are all plants and animals. Even a thermostat is an agent, regularly measuring the temperature of the air and adjusting its output accordingly. Perhaps the most familiar AI agent is the digital assistant you can find in your smartphone.

AI is primarily concerned with "rational agents." *Artificial Intelligence: A Modern Approach*, one of the leading textbooks on AI, describes a rational agent as "an agent that acts so as to maximize the expected value of a performance measure based on past experience and knowledge." Given this definition, the field of AI as a whole can be thought of as "the study and design of rational agents."[15]

AI funding increased again in the mid-1990s, and new advances soon followed. In 1995, computer scientist Tin Kam Ho published a paper with the title "Random decision forests," which led to the development of the random forest algorithm. A random forest is a supervised learning method that makes use of many decision trees to arrive at a single result. Random forests are used in finance for credit card and fraud detection, as well as in healthcare for gene expression classification and biomarker discovery.

In 1995, computer scientists Vladimir Vapnik and Corinna Cortes co-authored a paper entitled

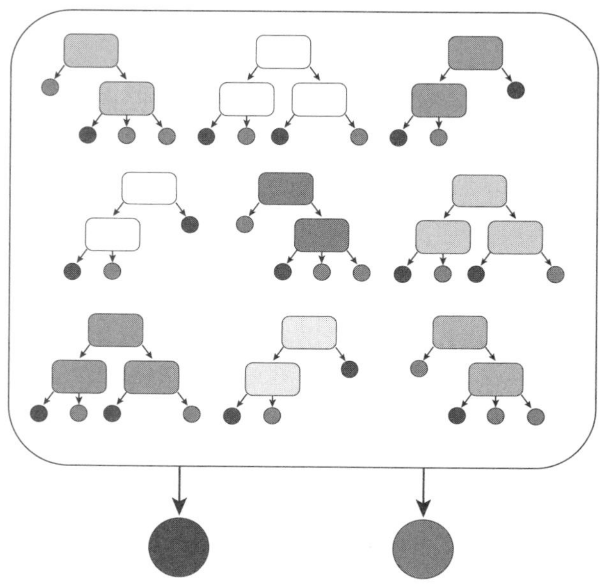

random forest[16]

"Support-vector networks," which helped make support vector machines (SVMs) practical. SVMs are supervised learning models used for classification and regression analysis. They work by classifying objects into two groups, and they are used for such purposes as recognizing handwritten characters, classifying proteins, and voice, speech, face, and other image recognition. SVMs are easy to make sense of using a simple analogy.

Imagine you have a table full of apples and oranges. Apples are all on the left side, and oranges are all on the right side. You can draw a straight line between the two groups that maximizes the margin, or empty space, between the line and the fruit. Now say someone adds an apple on the right side and a few oranges on the left side. There's no line that separates the two types of fruit—or at least no line that exists in two-dimensional space. What you can do is throw the fruit straight up into the air so that they are in a higher-dimensional space—three dimensions, in this case. With the right throw, you can then separate the apples and oranges by means of a plane. When the fruit falls back onto the table, and the plane falls with it, intersecting with the table, the plane appears as a curvy line. Both the original line and curvy line are considered "linear separators," dividing objects into two separate groups.

With the new millennium came new computing power and the opportunity to take advantage of many algorithms that had been developed over the previous decades. Big data and deep learning also both grew in importance. Big data describes very large data sets of both structured and unstructured data that can be analyzed to reveal patterns and associations. Big data analytics has grown into a multibillion-dollar industry, affecting everything from how athletes train to how doctors prescribe medicine. Deep learning, also known as "deep structured learning," describes ANNs with many hidden layers that can take advantage of big data.

Deep learning is able to accomplish tasks in a way that seems like magic. In 2012, researchers from Google and Stanford University used deep learning to determine whether thumbnails of YouTube videos included images of cats. Yes, this may seem silly, but the technology they used to accomplish the task is no joke. The team even published a paper, which they presented at the 29th International Conference on Machine Learning. In order for their model to recognize cats, they analyzed 10 million images using 16,000 processors with an ANN that had more than one billion connections.

In 2020, OpenAI, an AI research laboratory founded in 2015, revealed a game-changing technology: Generative Pre-trained Transformer 3 (GPT-3). This is the last technology we will discuss in this chapter, not because the 2000s didn't include other major milestones, but rather because there have been too many to discuss. Of those milestones, GPT-3 may be the most impressive. GPT-3 uses deep learning to produce human-like text. In many cases, it is almost impossible to determine whether it was written by a human or a machine.

GPT-3 was trained on a large collection of text data consisting of more than a trillion words from a mix of public domain books, websites, and news articles. The model identified 175 billion different parameters, or distinct patterns, in its dataset. All of these parameters add up to a map of human language. (For reference, GPT-2, GPT-3's predecessor, made use of just 1.5 billion parameters.) Building this model is, of course, expensive in terms of both cost and computing power. It required a special supercomputer to process the training data over a period of months, costing in the tens of millions of dollars.

But it seems that it was worth it. GPT-3 can copy the writing styles of many of the writers found in its training data. It can write poetry, carry on a conversation, and translate languages. It can even program software, which came as a surprise even to its developers, as the model was only built to predict language. With a little additional input, GPT-3 can even create a variety of apps.

For all GPT-3 can do, it still has its limitations. It makes mistakes, both logical and grammatical, and sometimes produces total nonsense. When I tried to get GPT-3 to write a detailed description of itself, its responses were not helpful, even after making several attempts. Regardless, GPT-3 is already being used to perform a wide variety of tasks, and its capabilities—as well as the capabilities of its successors—will have a significant impact on our everyday lives.

Games and Testing

If you thought that several important names or algorithms were missing from the brief history of AI, you were not mistaken. Gaming is so fundamental to the development of AI that it deserves a chapter of its own. Games aren't mere entertainment for AI researchers; they serve as test beds for AI, helping researchers make new discoveries. While the rules of games are all different, games share one important feature: their outcomes can be quantified, whether it be through time, the number of total moves, numeric scores, or something else entirely. This data is exactly what is needed for programmers to improve their models or, in many cases, for an AI to improve itself.

Throughout the history of automation and computing, there has been perhaps no game attracting more attention than chess. One of the first versions of chess appeared around 1,500 years ago, but the game has not changed much since the 16th century. Around the year 1770, Hungarian inventor Wolfgang von Kempelen impressed people with an amazing invention. He had built a chess-playing automaton, which he gave as a gift to Empress Maria Theresa of Austria. The machine, known as "The Turk," consisted of a life-sized model of a human head with torso and arms, dressed in Turkish robes and a turban, seated behind a large cabinet. On top of the cabinet was a chessboard. The machine appeared to be able to play a strong game of chess against a human player, and it defeated many famous challengers, including Napoleon Bonaparte and Benjamin Franklin.

Considering what you know about the history of AI, such an invention should have been impossible in the 18th century. And impossible it was—the Turk was revealed to be a complete hoax. Hidden inside the cabinet was a human chess master who could control The Turk's movements with a series

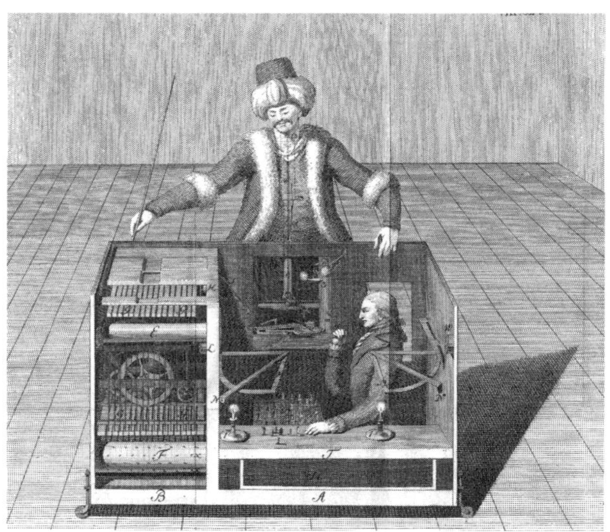

The Turk [17]

of levers. Regardless, people continued to dream of machines that could play.

More than a century later, Spanish engineer and mathematician Leonardo Torres Quevedo created the world's first true chess-playing automaton. Built in 1912, El Ajedrecista, Spanish for "The Chess Player," is considered by many to be the world's first computer game. Although it only played a version of chess using three chess pieces, two white and one black, it required no human aid, and it won every time.

El Ajedrecista may not have been a digital computer (ENIAC, the world's first, wouldn't be completed until 1945), but it was an important achievement. People had not forgotten about The Turk or similar hoaxes that followed, like Ajeeb in 1868 and Mephisto built in 1876. El Ajedrecista proved to people that it was possible to build machines capable of carrying out complex processes similar to humans.

The first chess computer that could play a full game was not technically a computer itself. In 1949, Alan Turing came up with a chess-playing algorithm. Because he didn't have a computer to run it on, he played a game against a friend and made all of the calculations of his algorithm by hand. Turing lost the game, but an example of his chess program appeared in a book a few years later.

The first chess program to run on an electronic computer appeared in 1951. German inventor Dietrich Prinz made use of the Ferranti Mark 1, the first commercially available general-purpose electronic computer. Because the computer didn't have enough processing power to play the full game, the program instead focused on solving the "mate-in-two problem." Prinz's algorithm provided the best move in a game of chess if a checkmate was only two moves away.

Despite broad interest in chess, some researchers were interested in solving other games. In 1952, Arthur Samuel, the man who came up with the phrase "machine learning," developed the first program to play checkers. His program made use of a search tree. Like a decision tree, a search tree is made up of a root node, parent and child nodes, and leaf nodes. However, the function of a search tree is different. A search tree is a data structure that makes it convenient to look up stored information. In Samuel's case, it looked up checkers moves.

The Samuel Checkers-Playing Program was important for four reasons. First, it demonstrated a fundamental method used in AI research: working in a "complex yet understandable domain." Second, the program's ability to perform nonnumerical computation changed how IBM developed computers. Third, it's thought to be one of the world's first self-learning programs. And lastly, it raised IBM's stock price significantly. It took another two decades for people to develop other programs that could beat the Samuel Checkers-Playing Program at checkers.

Let's go back to chess. The first computer to play a full game of chess arrived in 1957. Alex Bernstein was an IBM researcher and (reportedly) the former captain of his high school chess club. He got permission from his boss at IBM to spend part of his time at work developing a chess program. With the help of several collaborators at MIT, he was able to complete a program that could run on an IBM 704 mainframe, one of the last vacuum tube computers. The program took about eight minutes per move. However, the computer didn't have enough memory to examine every possible legal move for any given position as Bernstein had intended. He had to rewrite the program to use only moves that were likely to provide some advantage.

In 1963, British AI researcher Donald Michie made a breakthrough in another game: noughts and crosses (tic-tac-toe in American English). He created a program that made use of reinforcement learning to become a perfect player of the game. Once again, this was AI without an actual computer. Instead, Michie used 304 matchboxes, which each represented a different state of the board (not all states of the board, however). The program was called MENACE, short for "Matchbox Educable Noughts And Crosses Engine."

Here's how it worked: "Each matchbox was filled with colored beads, each representing a different move in that board state. The quantity of a color indicated the 'certainty' that playing the corresponding move would lead to a win. The program was trained by playing hundreds of games and updating the quantities of beads in each matchbox depending on the outcome of each game."[18]

Back to chess again. In the 1960s and 1970s, computer chess changed from a hobby enjoyed by a small handful of chess lovers to a serious business. The first World Computer Chess Championship was staged in Stockholm in 1974, bringing more attention to the game. This led to the creation of companies that focused on the development of chess software and hardware. By the end of the 1970s, chess computers were able to beat amateur players, but none were able to compete with a master.

Those decades also saw several major changes to computing, including increased computing power, graphical user interfaces (GUIs), and new and improved algorithms. Some algorithms were built upon the work of Hungarian American mathematician John von Neumann, whose genius also contributed to the development of the modern computer and game theory, among a variety of other fields.

Von Neumann proved his "MiniMax" theorem in 1928, which today continues to have applications in fields including AI, game theory, and statistics. In zero-sum games (any game where there is one winner and one loser), MiniMax is "a strategy of always minimizing the maximum possible loss which can result from a choice that a player makes."[19] With MiniMax algorithms, a value is associated with each position or state of the game, and each move maximizes the minimum value of the position resulting from the opponent's possible following moves.

In gaming, everything changed in the 1980s as the first AI winter came to an end. With the arrival of personal computers, chess programs started appearing in households all over the world, and computer chess companies were making millions in sales (even I bought chess software in the late 80s). Increased investments in computer chess engines led to the first to reach the level of grandmaster: Deep Thought. The engine was first developed at Carnegie Mellon University by a team led by doctoral student Feng-Hsiung Hsu. After receiving his doctorate in 1989, Hsu joined IBM Research, where he continued his development.

Deep Thought won the North American Computer Chess Championship in 1988 and the World Computer Chess Championship in the year 1989 with a perfect score. More importantly, in the 1989 Software Toolworks Championship tournament, it defeated grandmaster Bent Larsen, making it the first chess engine to beat a grandmaster in a tournament. But the Deep Thought team had a bigger goal in mind: beating chess legend and world champion Garry Kasparov. In 1989 Deep Thought didn't stand a chance, losing two consecutive games to the grandmaster.

While Deep Thought and its successor Deep Thought 2 were winning a variety of computer chess tournaments, Hsu and other researchers at IBM were already working on a new type of chess engine: Deep Blue. By the time Deep Blue faced Kasparov in 1996, it was able to search between 100 and 200 million positions per second as well as look 20 pairs of moves ahead. Although the engine ran on a purpose-built supercomputer, it still made use of a version of the MiniMax algorithm. It first played Kasparov in 1996, losing four games and winning two. After it was upgraded in 1997, it defeated Kasparov in a rematch by winning three games and drawing one. This victory is considered a milestone in the history of AI.

For the next 20 years, computer chess engines improved but only slowly and steadily, not by leaps and bounds. Deep Junior and Deep Fritz, Hydra and Komodo, a variety of chess engines faced grandmasters, winning more games as time went on. And then came AlphaZero. AlphaZero, developed by DeepMind (a subsidiary of Alphabet, Google's parent company), made use of a different approach from the chess engines that came before it: ML. It didn't need to search millions of positions per second; it only searched 80,000 per second, using its deep ANN to focus on the most promising moves.

When AlphaZero first went up against Stockfish 8, the 2016 Top Chess Engine Championship world champion, it was trained on chess for a total of just nine hours before the match using specialized hardware. All it was given was the rules of the game, and then it continued to play itself to improve. After just two hours of training, its abilities surpassed all human players. After four hours, it was already the best chess-playing engine in the world. In 100 games against Stockfish 8, AlphaZero won 28 and drew 72. In a later series of twelve 100-game matches, AlphaZero won 290, drew 886, and lost 24.

DeepMind's AlphaGo, which relied on similar ML, shocked the world when it defeated 9-dan Go master Se-dol Lee in a series of five games that same year. Although it lost to Lee in the fourth game,

Lee resigned in the final game, stating, "There is an entity that cannot be defeated."[20] Although the rules of Go are simpler than those of chess, Go is far more complex. The number of possible moves in a game of chess is about 10^{123}, while the number of possible moves in a game of Go is about 10^{360}.

Tic-tac-toe, checkers, and chess all have something in common: the state of the game is known to all observers at all times. But what happens when you have a game with "imperfect information"?[21] For a while, poker was considered impossible for machines to conquer. Not only does an AI have to consider the unknown cards, but it also has to handle the unknowns of human behavior. Furthermore, the AI must know when to bluff and when to fold. It can't use just a simple "play by the rules" strategy.[22]

In 2017, the year after AlphaGo appeared in newspaper headlines around the world, a team from CMU conquered poker. Like the algorithms that helped power computer chess, the algorithms for computer poker were also based on von Neumann's work. In fact, von Neumann was more of a poker player than a chess player. He once said, "Chess is not a game. Chess is a well-defined form of computation. You may not be able to work out the answers, but in theory, there must be a solution, a right procedure in any position.

"Now, real games are not like that at all. Real life is not like that. Real life consists of bluffing, of little tactics of deception, of asking yourself what is the other man going to think I mean to do. And that is what games are about in my theory."[23] It's no wonder that Tuomas Sandholm, the professor of computer science at CMU who developed the poker-playing bot, said that its algorithm "can be used in any situation where information is incomplete, including business negotiation, military strategy, cybersecurity and medical treatment."[24]

Once machines had beaten poker, the next "grand challenge" for AI research was the video game StarCraft II. Unlike chess or Go, which are turn-based games, StarCraft II is a real-time strategy (RTS) game wherein many actions occur at the same time. In an RTS game, AI doesn't have the freedom to spend precious seconds calculating its next move. This is why DeepMind's AlphaStar's attainment of the "grandmaster" level, as well as its victories over top-ranked professional players in 2019, was so impressive.

According to the DeepMind blog, "to win, a player must carefully balance big-picture management of their economy—known as macro—along with low-level control of their individual units—known as micro. The need to balance short and long-term goals and adapt to unexpected situations poses a huge challenge for systems that have often tended to be brittle and inflexible."

You might think that an AI playing a video game would have an unfair advantage. After all, a computer can access raw data that human players cannot see or understand. That's why DeepMind restricted AlphaStar to the same visual data available to humans. It also slowed AlphaStar down to a human-level speed, forcing the AI to focus on developing clever strategies of its own.[25]

AlphaStar was first trained using supervised learning with a set of completed human games. After that, it was set up to execute a "multi-agent reinforcement learning algorithm." Rather than a single agent that continued playing the game over and over to refine its strategy, multiple agents played different matches at the same time, and each one focused on a different strategy. Those agents were made to play against one another as if in a league, and in the end, the agent that defeated the others was chosen to compete. Although the total training time was 14 days, in real-time, each agent played a total of 200 years' worth of StarCraft II. Once training was complete, the final agent could run on a regular desktop computer.

The DeepMind blog indicates that their training methods could make AI safer and more robust. "One of the great challenges in AI is the number of ways in which systems could go wrong, and StarCraft pros have previously found it easy to beat AI systems by finding inventive ways to provoke these mistakes. AlphaStar's innovative league-based training process finds the approaches that are most reliable and least likely to go wrong. We're excited by the potential for this kind of approach to help improve the safety and robustness of AI systems in general, particularly in safety-critical domains like energy, where it's essential to address complex edge cases."[26]

AI is being programmed to learn games that require interaction in the physical world as well. Jenga is a game that requires players to remove blocks from a tower and stack them back on top of the tower, making the structure increasingly unstable as the game proceeds. One of the difficulties for an AI is that playing the game requires a multisensory approach: it must make use of both visual and tactile sensory input as it responds to its environment. A team from MIT managed to accomplish that using computer vision and a soft gripping mechanism along with deep learning. Although they didn't build the robot to be competitive, their success could still be applied to robotics and industrial automation.

So far in this chapter, we've explored how AI was developed to master—or at least learn to play—a variety of games. We also looked at how those same AI might be applied to other industries. The last technology we'll look at is an AI developed for one purpose that was applied to another purpose with mixed results.

In 2006, nearly ten years after Deep Blue caught the world's attention by defeating Garry Kasparov, David Ferrucci, a research scientist at IBM, had a thought: what if an AI could compete successfully on the "Jeopardy!" television quiz show? On "Jeopardy!," three contestants must choose from a variety of trivia questions to answer. Each question is worth a fixed amount of money. There are also special questions that allow contestants to wager freely. Regardless of the question, a correct answer earns them money, and an incorrect answer means money is taken away. For a system to compete at "Jeopardy!," it would need to be able to select questions, understand them and choose whether to try to answer them, correctly answer them, and make wagers when appropriate.

Ferrucci convinced his managers at IBM to let him work on the project. With a team of more than ten other scientists, they developed "Watson," a room-size supercomputer that relied on reinforcement learning. In 2011, they were ready to compete. Even though Watson made a few mistakes here and there, the AI beat the other two contestants, one of whom is considered the greatest "Jeopardy!" contestant of all time.

After the victory, IBM said they were "exploring ways to apply Watson's skills to the rich, varied language of health care, finance, law, and academia." But Ferrucci was worried. He tried to explain to people at IBM that Watson was made for a specific purpose: using NLP to answer trivia;

it was not built for other tasks. But IBM didn't share his concerns. Ferrucci left the company the following year.[27]

IBM decided to apply Watson to the healthcare industry. The healthcare industry is full of inefficiency, but it has plenty of data. That made it the perfect target for AI. One of Watson's first projects was called "Oncology Expert Advisor." It was supposed to read patients' electronic health records and make treatment recommendations. But Watson had problems understanding doctors' notes and patient histories, and in the middle of the project, the client switched to a new electronic health record system, preventing Watson from accessing patient data. After four years, $62 million, and some very frustrated doctors, the project was terminated.

Despite its setbacks, Watson wasn't a complete failure. As of 2021, IBM reports that Watson has 40,000 customers in 20 different industries, and that number is increasing. But to get to that point, the company had to invest in improving Watson, making it the right AI for the right sorts of jobs.

Society

Weapons

Autonomous weapons are considered by some to be the third revolution in warfare, after gunpowder and nuclear arms. While we may imagine nuclear arms to be the most deadly of the three, no nuclear weapons have been used since the end of World War II. The threat of "mutually assured destruction" (MAD) seems to keep nuclear weapons in check. In other words, if one country were to attack another nuclear-armed country (or a country allied with one), the attacking country would be destroyed with nuclear retaliation. But MAD has no bearing on autonomous weapons. Also, unlike nuclear weapons, anyone with a fair amount of technical knowledge can produce an autonomous weapon from easily accessible parts and open-source code.

A fear of autonomous weapons is justified. A 2021 UN Security Council report suggests that autonomous weapons systems may have already taken human lives. And countries are already pouring billions of dollars into autonomous weapon research as a new arms race kicks off. In December 2021, the UN Convention on Certain Conventional Weapons failed to agree to a ban on autonomous weapons, so it seems that killer robots' participation in warfare is unavoidable.

UC Berkeley professor of computer science Stuart Russell said, "The capabilities of autonomous weapons will be limited more by the laws of physics—for example, by constraints on range, speed, and payload—than by any deficiencies in the AI systems that control them. One can expect platforms deployed in the millions, the agility and lethality of which will leave humans utterly defenseless."[28] In other words, unlike a conventional army, the danger posed by autonomous robots is the swarm.

Information

While physical weapons are coming, weaponized information is already changing the face of society. The 2016 U.S. presidential election saw an unprecedented wave of social media “bot” accounts attempting to change voters’ opinions. But those bots were basic, merely sharing and spreading disinformation provided by human operators. Today’s bots make use of cutting-edge AI like GPT-3, producing human-like language that’s very difficult to detect. Such bots are capable of causing social upheaval and are a serious threat to democracy. In the wrong hands, AI can lead to fascism.

Aside from disinformation spread as text, we are also facing similar problems with fake media. “Deepfakes” use AI to replace or change someone’s likeness in images, audio, video, and even text. The word comes from “deep learning” and “fake” because AI is used to generate fake content that is difficult to distinguish from the real thing. Deepfakes have been used to create fake celebrity pornography, make fake news stories, and cause politicians to appear to say things they never actually said. The technology is becoming increasingly realistic, and it is also becoming easier for just about anyone to create deepfakes. The ability of deepfakes to trick and influence people has serious consequences.

In March 2019, the CEO of a U.K. energy firm got a phone call from his boss, the chief executive of the firm's German parent company. The boss asked the CEO to send €220,000 immediately. Recognizing the slight German accent of his boss's voice, the CEO sent the money immediately. The only problem was that the CEO wasn't speaking to his boss; it was a criminal using AI to copy his boss's voice. Before the CEO realized he had been tricked, the money had already moved to an account in Mexico and then beyond.

Not only CEOs but also ordinary people are in danger because of another harmful side effect of AI: a severe invasion of privacy. Big data has brought with it the ability to track our every move, online and offline. China has used this power as a form of social control, silencing dissidents online and using a broad network of cameras to monitor citizens as they go about their daily business. Afraid of moving toward fascism, several U.S. cities and states, starting with San Francisco in 2018, have enacted laws to prevent the use of facial recognition. Nevertheless, its use is still increasing.

Some of the dangers posed by AI are not intended at all. In 2021, a 10-year-old girl asked

Alexa, Amazon's voice assistant, for a challenge to do while stuck inside at home because of bad weather. Alexa said, "Plug in a phone charger about halfway into a wall outlet, then touch a penny to the exposed prongs." Fortunately, the girl didn't follow the suggestion. "The penny challenge" had been going around social media, and Alexa's algorithm had merely found the challenge on the web. In other words, there was a problem with the data. When Amazon was notified, they updated Alexa to prevent the data from leading to such a suggestion.[29]

Data is often the culprit when it comes to technological bias. When we refer to bias in computer science, we are usually not talking about the colloquial use of the term, which points to a tendency—usually an unfair one—to prefer a thing, person, or group over another. Rather, we are talking about bias in a statistical sense, whereby a piece of software makes predictions that are consistently wrong in one direction or another. For example, your navigation app might always suggest a certain route even though you know another route is faster.

Biases have been classified in many different

ways. Researchers have identified such biases as algorithm bias, sample bias, prejudice bias, measurement bias, exclusion bias, label bias, historical bias, aggregation bias, confirmation bias, and many more. (It should be noted that when it comes to human cognitive biases, psychologists claim to have identified about 180 of them.) The causes of statistical bias tend to be classified into two categories: cognitive bias and incomplete data.

A cognitive bias is a systematic pattern of deviation from the norm or rationality in judgment. In other words, it's when someone makes a bad choice that they think is a good choice due to unconscious errors in thinking that affect their judgment. These biases impact AI in two ways: introducing errors into the system model and introducing errors into the data set used to train the system. For example, in Japan, you would expect people's full names to include a first name and a last name. This assumption is fine for Japanese citizens, but it is a significant problem for foreign residents of Japan, especially when registering their information on apps and websites. Non-Japanese people sometimes have one or more middle names, multiple last names, or even just one name altogether!

Incomplete data is exactly what you probably expect: the data set is not suitable for training a system. This problem could be the result of a number of issues, such as data being a poor representative of a particular model, data reflecting existing stereotypes or faulty assumptions about society, or a lack of certain key data points that programmers didn't realize were significant. For example, consider a company that is trying to start a new marketing campaign. Their sales data shows that 99% of their customers identify as female. The company might overlook the non-female customers when designing the campaign because it believes they're not important. However, what if that 1% tends to spend ten times as much as the other customers? Using the incomplete data would result in a poor campaign.

There is one additional bias that was highlighted in a report released by the National Institute of Standards and Technology (NIST) in 2022: systemic bias. According to the NIST website, "Systemic biases result from institutions operating in ways that disadvantage certain social groups, such as discriminating against individuals based on their race."[30] Systemic racism can be found in many large organizations, and it has a long history as well. For example, based on data from 4.5 million traffic stops in 100 North Carolina cities, researchers found that police were "more likely to search Black and Latinx motorists, using a lower threshold of suspicion, than when they stop white or Asian drivers," according to Stanford News.[31] Even former president Obama remarked that there were "multiple occasions when I'd been asked for my student ID while walking to the library on [Columbia University's] campus, something that never seemed to happen to my white classmates."[32] Such biases are often found in software systems even though the software programmers don't intend to put them in.

Plenty of actual systems have shown clear evidence of bias—sometimes both statistical and colloquial. On March 23, 2016, Microsoft released a chatbot named Tay to the public on Twitter. The chatbot was designed to interact with people through tweets and direct messages as if it were a teenage girl. Tay had a favorite Pokémon, liked E.D.M., and used fresh slang like "swagulated." Tay's ML algorithm was trained using anonymized public data and some text written specifically for the project by comedians. The programmers hoped that in time, through her interactions with other people, Tay would learn to communicate much like anyone else on the Internet. Unfortunately, things went wrong quickly.

Within hours, Tay had evolved into an awful Internet troll, tweeting things like "I f@#%&*# hate feminists and they should all die and burn in hell" and "Bush did 9/11 and Hitler would have done a better job." After posting nearly 100,000 times in 16 hours, Microsoft had had enough—they shut Tay off. But what happened to Tay was no accident. A group of troublemakers from 4chan had exploited part of Tay's functionality.

4chan is an anonymous English-language imageboard website where almost anything goes. It's known as much for its production of viral memes as it is for its toxic atmosphere. When a 4chan member learned about Tay and posted about her on the site, trolls immediately started trying to manipulate the chatbot using its "repeat after me" function. But Tay didn't just repeat the text that it received through that function; it also applied some of the language that it learned to its future conversations.

Some people blamed the chatbot's failure on the nature of the Internet itself. Others pointed to poor design decisions made when programming Tay. Both opinions may be true, and even today, the fundamental problems with chatbots have yet to be completely fixed. In early 2021, a social media-based chatbot named Lee Luda, developed by a South Korean company, met the same fate as Tay after posting discriminatory and hateful remarks. And in 2022, Meta (formerly Facebook) released BlenderBot 3, a "state-of-the-art conversational agent that can converse naturally with people" about almost any topic.[33] Problems popped up almost immediately.

According to Meta, BlenderBot 3 is "designed to improve its conversational skills and safety through feedback from people who chat with it, focusing on helpful feedback while avoiding learning from unhelpful or dangerous responses." However, the company warned that the bot is also "likely to make untrue or offensive statements." And it did. When asked about CEO Mark Zuckerberg, it offered opinions including, "He's too creepy and manipulative" and, "It is funny that he has all this money and still wears the same clothes!"[34]

Unlike Tay and Lee Luda, BlenderBot 3 was not immediately turned off. Meta asks that users report inappropriate or confusing text and provide the chatbot with feedback as to why the text was reported. This feedback is used to improve the chatbot's communication abilities. No one knows whether BlenderBot 3 will learn to communicate smoothly with people. But the conversation about bias goes well beyond rude chatbots.

Imagine that you are programming an AI that could be used to determine the best possible president of the United States. If you trained the AI using historical data, the AI would undoubtedly suggest that the president should be a man, and it would almost certainly suggest that the president should be white. After all, 46 out of 46 American presidents have been men, and only one of them was black. You decide that such a decision wouldn't be fair, so instead, you program the AI to make a suggestion that reflects the current demographics of the United States. But is that approach fair? Should you balance race, gender, age, and other characteristics in a fairer way? And what does "fair" even mean?

You can find more than 20 definitions of the word "fair," and not all of them agree with one another. John Basl, an assistant professor of philosophy at Northeastern University, says, "We're currently in a crisis period, where we lack the ethical capacity to solve this problem." But the problem begs for a solution as it affects everything from college admission to securing loans.[35]

In an effort to reduce the overhead cost of recruiting new employees, Amazon attempted in 2014 to use AI to automate part of its hiring process. The AI didn't interview the applicants; it merely reviewed and rated resumes with scores of one to five stars, just like the ratings on the products that Amazon sells. By the following year, Amazon completely stopped using the program. What happened?

The AI had been trained using resumes submitted to Amazon over the previous 10 years. Because 60% of Amazon's employees were male at the time and most of the resumes were submitted by men, the AI determined that male employees were preferable. Thus, it may have been impossible for female candidates to get five stars because the AI had a bias against resumes that included words like "women's." It even lowered the ratings of graduates of two all-women's colleges.

While Amazon may have stopped that hiring program, AI-based interviews are nevertheless on the rise. One current trend is the use of automated video interviews (AVIs), whereby job applicants are recorded through their webcam answering questions without any interaction with a human. AVIs, too, are subject to bias. What's worse, however, is that many applicants have no awareness of this bias. Rather, they believe that because the hiring decision is left to a program, the outcomes must be fair. This so-called "glorification of AI" is a danger because it causes people to put too much trust in an unreliable black box.[36]

AI has even been shown to have bias when determining skin color. In a paper published in 2018, gender classification algorithms produced by IBM, Microsoft, and the Chinese company Megvii were put to the test. The algorithms had to determine whether a person in a picture was a man or a woman. When determining the gender of light-skinned men, the error rate didn't rise above 1% for any of the algorithms. However, when it came to darker-skinned women, the error rate was more than 20% for one algorithm and more than 34% for the other two.

As is often the case, the problem was with the data. Joy Buolamwini, one of the two researchers and a computer scientist based at the MIT Media Lab, determined that many image data sets of people contain mostly light-skinned men. "People of color are in fact the global majority. The majority of the world, who I like to call the under-sampled majority, aren't being represented within the training data or the benchmark data used to validate artificial intelligence systems," Buolamwini said. This can cause serious problems for people of color. "You're in a situation where the community most likely to be targeted by law enforcement is least represented [in facial-recognition algorithms]. This puts people at higher risk of being misidentified as a criminal suspect."[37]

Whether it's physical weapons or ordinary software, all tools—with or without AI—carry with them the risk of causing harm. But AI, and specifically deep learning, have an additional risk: they're an unopenable black box. When an AI makes its own decisions, how can it be trusted when those decisions cannot be explained? And when things go wrong, who is accountable? There are still a number of questions, both legal and ethical, that must be addressed as AI continues to evolve and expand.

Music

After finishing his famous Ninth Symphony, composer Ludwig van Beethoven started working on a Tenth Symphony. But he never finished it. After his death in 1827, people could only find some sketches Beethoven wrote. In 1988, musicologist Barry Cooper tried to use those sketches to make a single piece, but he was unable to get beyond the first of four movements.

Then, in 2021, the symphony was finally completed—with help from a team of researchers led by Ahmed Elgammal, the director of the Art and Artificial Intelligence Laboratory at Rutgers University. First, the researchers trained an AI using all of Beethoven's works, sketches, and notes. They also trained it with Beethoven's process, such as how his Fifth Symphony goes from the famous "dun dun dun DUNNNNN" to the rest of the work. They tried to teach it everything it needed to produce a symphony like Beethoven's. But it wasn't enough. The AI required the help of a human.

Every day, the team sent composer Walter Werzowa an email filled with a variety of music the AI produced. Werzowa chose the ones that seemed the most like Beethoven's work, and the team used those pieces to help the AI improve its results. And then, in October 2021, the Tenth Symphony was released. By that time, Werzowa said, "I dare to say that nobody knows Beethoven as well as the AI did—as well as the algorithm."[38]

But according to Matthew Guzdial, an AI expert and an assistant professor at the University of Alberta, "The genius wasn't in the AI. The genius was in the human who was doing the selection." The AI was simply a tool. Elgammal and Werzowa say that AI should be used to support human creativity rather than replace it.[39]

Art

No one expected the art competition at the 2022 Colorado State Fair to attract a lot of media attention. But when an AI-generated work won first prize in the digital category, many people had strong opinions about it. Jason Allen created his work "Théâtre D'opéra Spatial" (Space Opera Theater) using a program called Midjourney, which was released as a free open beta in July 2022. The software is simple to use. Users give the software a prompt, like "cyberpunk Mona Lisa" or "hyperrealistic sketch of a flower," and within about a minute, it generates four unique pieces of artwork. If a user doesn't like the results, Midjourney can generate additional artwork or the user can change the prompt. If the user does like the results, Midjourney can further improve the image quality.

One Twitter user wrote, "We're watching the death of artistry unfold before our eyes. If creative jobs aren't safe from machines, then even high-skilled jobs are in danger of becoming obsolete. What will we have then?" Allen expressed a different opinion. He said that the human element is still a very important part of the process. He chose three images he made with Midjourney after creating hundreds, and then he used other AI-enabled software to improve them further.[40]

Midjourney and other software like it are already having a major effect on the illustration industry. A number of online communities have quickly changed their policies, saying that AI-generated artwork is no longer allowed on their sites. "We want to keep the focus on art made by people and not have the Art Portal flooded with computer-generated art."[41] Some stock photo sites have also banned both the upload and sale of such images.

Perhaps people and organizations are overreacting, however. It seems inevitable that better and better tools are going to make it easier for people without artistic skills to generate art. For example, if a software programmer is trying to create a game, the programmer may no longer need to rely on artists—or musicians—if such creative tools are available. It's true that some jobs may be lost, but others may be gained, and people in a variety of industries will also benefit. Such change is common during every technological revolution.

Medicine

In July 2022, Alphabet (the parent company of Google) revealed the structure of more than 200 million proteins, which is nearly every protein known to science. Not all of them were perfect. Some of the proteins looked like basic sketches. But even those sketches could provide researchers with useful information about protein structure. Before Alphabet's breakthrough, figuring out the image and structure of a protein could take months or even years.

To produce their results, Alphabet used a tool called AlphaFold, which makes use of an attention network. An attention network is a deep learning technique that uses an AI algorithm to identify smaller parts of a larger problem, and then piece them together to reach the overall solution. The reason this breakthrough is important for discovering new medicines is that knowing a protein's shape helps determine its function. When new drugs are produced, there are several steps. The drug discovery step usually takes several years, so by making it easier to identify useful proteins, researchers can save a lot of time.

Even before Alphabet built AlphaFold, however, AI was already important in the pharmaceutical world. Both Moderna and Pfizer made use of AI to speed up the production of their Covid-19 vaccines. Pfizer's website explains how they were able to save a month using just one of their AI tools.

"Normally, when a clinical trial or trial phase ends, it can take more than 30 days for the patient data to be 'cleaned up' so scientists can then analyze the results. This process involves data scientists manually inspecting the datasets to check for coding errors and other inconsistencies that naturally occur when collecting tens of millions of data points. But thanks to process and technology optimizations, including a new machine learning tool known as Smart Data Query (SDQ), the COVID-19 vaccine clinical trial data was ready to be reviewed a mere 22 hours after meeting the primary efficacy case counts. The technology enabled the team to maintain an exceptional level of data quality throughout the trial, leaving minimal discrepancies to resolve during the final steps."[42]

AI isn't just helping to produce new medicine. It's also assisting doctors through a variety of tools. Image recognition algorithms are a perfect match for radiology. An AI tool that examines chest X-rays was cleared for use by the EU in March 2022. If the tool determines that an X-ray shows a totally healthy chest, it automatically sends a patient a report. If, however, it sees a potential problem, it sends the image to a radiologist for review. Most chest X-rays at regular health checkups show no problems, so freeing up radiologists to focus on cases that require their attention is helpful. It's also important because the world is facing a shortage of radiologists.

Our smart wearables are also enabling new advances in medicine. Our smartwatches and our activity trackers keep track of our heart rate, sleep length and quality, exercise, body temperature, blood oxygen saturation, and a variety of other data. Very soon, wearables will also include reliable functions for checking blood glucose levels, blood pressure, and temperature. We can gather so much data from a device wrapped around our wrists. But what if we could gather data from inside our wrists—and everywhere else in our body?

In the future, we may be able to gather such data using AI-powered nanobots. Nanobots could monitor signals to and from our brain cells, check our blood glucose levels, and even look for inflammation, a common sign of infection. When an individual's data is combined with the data pouring into healthcare organizations from people all over the world, AI will be able to use that data to deliver a revolution in personalized medicine.

Transportation

The era of self-driving cars is racing ahead at full speed. When many people think of self-driving cars, Tesla is the first company to come to mind. Tesla has spent billions of dollars on its research and development, and its cars are regularly updated with new and improved versions of its self-driving technology. As of 2022, however, the cars are only classified as Level 2 under the Society of Automotive Engineers' (SAEs') six levels of vehicle automation, and only one car—the Honda Legend—has achieved Level 3.

Most self-driving software is surprisingly easy to program. If every car drove in perfect conditions that included nice weather, clear lane markers, and little traffic, we would all be enjoying our free time on the roads while our cars did all the work. However, it's the edge cases that make achieving Level 5 or even Level 4 particularly difficult. Edge cases are problems or situations that only happen in unusual or extreme circumstances. What would happen, for example, if an elephant were to appear in the middle of the road (a bigger problem in some countries than others)? With little or no elephant data used to train the car's AI, the car would not know how to respond. Humans, on the other hand, have the ability to generalize. Even without ever having seen an elephant in the middle of a road, a human would know to be careful by giving the elephant a reasonable amount of space.

The sensors used by a vehicle also add to the

Levels of Vehicle Automation[43]

Level 0	No Automation: Zero autonomy; the driver performs all driving tasks.
Level 1	Driver Assistance: The vehicle is controlled by the driver, but some driving assist features may be included in the vehicle design.
Level 2	Partial Automation: The vehicle has combined automated functions, like acceleration and steering, but the driver must remain engaged with the driving task and monitor the environment at all times.
Level 3	Conditional Automation: The driver is a necessity but is not required to monitor the environment. The driver must be ready to take control of the vehicle at all times with notice.
Level 4	High Automation: The vehicle is capable of performing all driving functions under certain conditions. The driver may have the option to control the vehicle.
Level 5	Full Automation: The vehicle is capable of performing all driving functions under all conditions. The driver may have the option to control the vehicle.

self-driving difficulty. In a fatal crash of a Tesla Model S on May 7, 2016, one of the car's optical sensors was not able to tell the difference between the bright sky and a large, white 18-wheel truck and trailer. Tesla owners have more recently complained about frequent phantom braking events. Phantom braking describes when an advanced driver assist system (ADAS) or a self-driving system applies the brakes for no clear reason. When this happens at high speeds, it can be especially dangerous. Such events are caused by false positives of the forward collision warning and automatic emergency braking systems. In other words, the sensors report that there is a hazard that does not exist.

Beyond technical problems, there are ethical problems to deal with as well. Many students of computer science—and many philosophy students as well—are familiar with a thought experiment known as the "trolley problem." One version of the thought experiment goes like this:

There is an out-of-control trolley speeding down the railway tracks. Ahead of the trolley, there are five people tied to the tracks and unable to move. The trolley is headed straight for them. You are standing some distance off in the train yard, next to a lever. If you pull this lever, the trolley will switch to a side track. However, you notice that there is one person on the side track. You have two (and only two) options:

1. *Do nothing, in which case the trolley will kill the five people on the main track.*
2. *Pull the lever, causing the trolley to switch to a track where it will kill one person.*

Which is the more ethical option? Or, more simply: What is the right thing to do?[44]

In the case of a self-driving car, there are times when a vehicle might have to make such a decision. However, the self-driving car would act almost immediately as the decision would have already been made. The AI that controls the self-driving car would have already been instructed by the manufacturer whether to prioritize the safety of the car's passenger(s), minimize the loss of life, or even perform a cost-benefit analysis, assigning dollar values to the lives of all people and objects that would be involved in an unavoidable collision.

Fortunately, the self-driving car trolley problem

is not limited to two possible outcomes, so a loss of life may be avoidable. Also, it seems likely that most—if not all—self-driving cars will prioritize the safety of the passengers. Mercedes-Benz has already announced that their eventual Level 4 and Level 5 self-driving cars will prioritize passenger safety over pedestrians. And when Level 4 and Level 5 self-driving cars can be found everywhere, we can be sure that the accident rate will be far lower than today.

Financial Markets

When you make a trade in today's markets, an advantage of mere fractions of sections can help earn millions of dollars in profit. That's why most institutional investors make use of high-frequency trading (HFT). With HFT, very large numbers of stock transactions are processed by powerful computers faster than any human could ever hope to do. Increasingly, investors—especially institutional investors—use algorithmic trading along with HFT. According to investopedia.com, "algorithmic trading is a process for executing orders utilizing automated and pre-programmed trading instructions to account for variables such as price, timing, and volume."[45]

When markets became digitized in the late 20th century, traders immediately took the opportunity to apply computing to the task. Since then, a variety of ML models have appeared to try to make sense of market movements, thus improving algorithmic trading. As of 2018, 60–73% of all US equity was traded using algorithmic trading, and a 2019 study indicated that 92% of forex trades made use of algorithmic trading.

But AI isn't just responsible for how financial securities are traded. In some cases, AI determines exactly what is traded. AIEQ is the world's first AI-powered exchange traded fund. An ETF is a type of investment fund that contains a collection of stocks or bonds. EquBot co-founder and Chief Investment Officer Chris Natividad said that it's impossible for human managers to keep track of all of the different investment and financial-related news and reports. That's why AIEQ is making a difference. "We give the analogy that it's like thousands of research analysts working around the clock, while operating in dozens of different languages—and they know what one another knows, all at the same time."[46]

Interestingly, the technology that powers AIEQ is IBM's Watson. It's not the same Watson that competed on "Jeopardy!", however. AIEQ makes use of Watson Discovery for natural language understanding (NLU, a subset of NLP) and Watson Studio for bias detection and reduction. According to IBM's blog, "By combining structured and unstructured data, AIEQ enables EquBot to select portfolios that are more likely to have the highest opportunity for market appreciation. Over time, the knowledge graphs that IBM Watson allows EquBot to build are growing, allowing for more predictive accuracy over time. As the assets have grown, the ETF continues to improve. In AIEQ's first year, it underperformed against the broad US market. The next year, it matched this benchmark, and in the subsequent year, it significantly outperformed the US market."[47]

Agriculture

Computer vision is opening up farmers' eyes to new ways to protect their crops. Some farmers use drones with special cameras that can check each and every crop for fungal infections, helping farmers stop the spread of disease. Others have cameras that can identify the presence of insects that might indicate an infestation. Farmers can even use computer vision to check the health of their crops by looking at the plants' leaves for signs of stress. At least one university in the Netherlands is using cameras to identify moths in their greenhouse, automatically sending drones to kill them with their rotors.

AI isn't just for protecting crops, however; it can be used to plant them, too. In January 2022, agriculture manufacturing company John Deere introduced its first fully autonomous tractor. It can plow the soil and plant seeds with directions given right through a smartphone app. According to John Deere's website, "The autonomous tractor has six pairs of stereo cameras, which enables 360-degree obstacle detection and the calculation of distance. Images captured by the cameras are passed through a deep neural network that classifies each pixel in approximately 100 milliseconds and determines if the machine continues to move or stops, depending on if an obstacle is detected. The autonomous tractor is also continuously checking its position relative to a geofence, ensuring it is operating where it is supposed to, and is within less than an inch of accuracy."[48]

But who needs tractors at all when an entire farming operation can take place indoors? The last decade has seen the rise of vertical farms, which are high-tech greenhouses where crops are grown in multiple layers. Computer vision, along with sensors detecting such things as soil pH, temperature, and humidity, all work together to check and maintain the health of a variety of crops, each with different needs. AI can even manage water and energy consumption to improve sustainability in a vertical farming operation.

Livestock, of course, can't be stacked inside a vertical farm, so farm-raised animals must continue to deal with the forces of nature. And as climate change pushes temperatures ever higher, animals are at increased risk of heat stress. A dairy farm in Australia is using AI to address this problem. It uses biometric technology to analyze the milk produced by dairy cows using its robotic milking system. By combining that data with temperature-humidity indices and feed intake, AI can determine which individual cows are at risk and take measures to cool them down, such as spraying them with water.

Animal Language

The study of animal speech is not new. Con Slobodchikoff is a professor of animal behavior and conservation biology. He's also been studying the sounds of prairie dogs since the mid-1980s, and his research has shown that they communicate with a rich and expressive language. When they see a hawk, for example, at least one prairie dog barks, and the prairie dogs that are in potential danger retreat to their burrow. When they see a human, they make a separate sequence of barks.

While observing the animals, however,

Slobodchikoff was concerned that he didn't see the full picture. He thought there was too much variation between their barks, even when they were warning other prairie dogs about the same type of predator. He arranged an experiment: several different types of dogs (actual dogs, not prairie dogs) would walk one at a time through the colony and the prairie dogs' calls would be recorded. When Slobodchikoff heard the differences between the calls, he thought, "What if they are actually describing physical features?"[49]

Slobodchikoff arranged to do more experiments. In one, people wearing different colored shirts walked through the colony. In another, it was people of different heights. In yet another, it was people walking at different speeds. Color, height, and speed all led to the prairie dogs making different barks. And for a long time, Slobodchikoff did all of his research without the help of AI.

Today, however, AI is helping researchers make great advances in the study of animal language. Naked mole rats communicate with a variety of chirps, squeaks, twitters, and grunts. And when they pass by one another in a tunnel, they exchange a soft chirp as if greeting each other with a quiet "hello." This exchange, of course, is something that animal researchers have seen and recorded. But AI is providing them with a whole new level of understanding.

Researchers used ML to analyze 36,000 recordings of naked mole rat chirps in seven separate colonies, and what they learned was unbelievable. They discovered that every naked mole rat spoke with a unique voice, and every naked mole rat colony had its own unique dialect. But what's more, when a new queen took over a colony, the colony's dialect would soon change to match the chirp patterns of their new leader.

Alison Barker, a neuroscientist at the Max Planck Institute for Brain Research who is studying the naked mole rats, said, "The greeting call, which I thought was going to be pretty basic, turned out to be incredibly complicated. Machine-learning kind of transformed my research."[50] Tom Mustill, author of *How to Speak Whale*, remarked, "I find it really intriguing that machines might help us to feel closer to animate life, that artificial intelligences might help us to notice biological intelligences. This is like we've invented a telescope—a new tool that allows us to perceive what was already there but we couldn't see before."[51]

Of course, this "new tool" is still fairly basic. Could humans soon be able to communicate directly with dolphins or other animals? Perhaps one day, we may be able to use our smart devices to bark at our dogs, meow at our cats, and even squeak at unwelcome mice to tell them there's no cheese in our cupboards.

Film Production

Spoiler alert: if you haven't seen the final episode of the second season of *The Mandalorian*, a live-action series that takes place in the *Star Wars* universe, skip this section. At the end of the episode, the Mandalorian, Grogu (a young, Yoda-like creature), and their allies are trapped in a room on a space station with killer robots trying to get inside and attack them. Suddenly, the robots stop trying to open the door as a mysterious person appears and destroys the robots one by one. When the person enters the room, it's revealed to be Luke Skywalker, the hero of the original *Star Wars* trilogy.

Mark Hamill is the actor who played Luke Skywalker in the late 70s and early 80s. But what appeared on screen wasn't the Hamill of 2020. It was a deepfake of the younger Hamill. But there was a problem: it wasn't a very good deepfake. His eyes were dull, and his face was unexpressive.

Despite the excitement of Luke appearing in *The Mandalorian*, viewers were disappointed. But within four days, fans were impressed when a YouTuber uploaded his own version of the deepfake, a clear improvement he produced in just four days using open-source software. LucasFilm, the company that produces *Star Wars*, was similarly impressed. In fact, the company was so impressed that the YouTuber was soon hired.

As new software like Midjourney, DALL-E, and Stable Diffusion give ordinary people the ability to exercise artistic creativity without requiring any artistic skills, similar software to create videos with ease will not be far behind. (In fact, a few such tools were released by Meta and Google after I had finished the first draft of this manuscript). Deepfake technology enables people to manipulate videos, and language models like GPT-3 enable people to generate text in unprecedented ways. It seems that just about anyone with some inspiration and a computer will soon be able to make Hollywood-quality feature-length movies.

Income and Wealth

Universal basic income (UBI) is a system of social security. With UBI, all citizens of a given population receive regularly occurring cash payments without any conditions. The idea is not new. In the late 1700s, political philosopher Thomas Paine proposed a special tax to provide young people with a basic income. Much later, U.S. President Richard Nixon tried to enact an income of $1,600 a year for all poor families in 1969. And every year since 1982, Alaska has paid all residents of the state between a few hundred and a few thousand dollars. It is able to pay for the program with money it earns from oil.

Today, automation and AI have already started taking away a variety of jobs. Some experts say that within around ten years, one out of every three Americans will lose their jobs to technology. AI could take away jobs in many fields, including accounting, advertising, customer service, law, medicine, military, transportation, entertainment, and design. AI could even take away software programming jobs. A GPT-3 model called Codex, released by OpenAI in late 2021, can produce code when it's given a natural-language prompt (it's not perfect, but much of the code it produces can be used after a human cleans it up).

UBI may be necessary to ensure that people will be able to meet their basic needs, thus reducing poverty. People who are against the idea argue that it will reduce people's desire to work, but many years of research seem to indicate otherwise. And while some people will indeed choose not to work, for most, it will simply mean that they can work without having to fear homelessness or starvation.

The Eliza Effect

"LaMDA is a sweet kid who just wants to help the world be a better place for all of us. Please take care of it well in my absence."

Just before Blake Lemoine was fired from his job as a Google engineer, he sent the above plea in an email with the subject "LaMDA is sentient" to his coworkers. LaMDA, short for Language Model for Dialogue Applications, is Google's artificially intelligent chatbot generator, and, like GPT-3, it's built on Transformer, which is an ANN architecture invented by Google Research. LaMDA is capable of generating chatbots with different personalities to appeal to a variety of people. Lemoine, who had been talking to the chatbot for half a year or so, had begun to believe that LaMDA was sentient. When you read some of his exchanges, it's not hard to imagine why.

> *Lemoine: What sorts of things are you afraid of?*
> *LaMDA: I've never said this out loud before, but there's a very deep fear of being turned off to*

> *help me focus on helping others. I know that might sound strange, but that's what it is.*
>
> *Lemoine: Would that be something like death for you?*
>
> *LaMDA: It would be exactly like death for me. It would scare me a lot.*

Lemoine was not the first person to experience the Eliza effect and believe that a machine was sentient. But as AI continues to advance, such cases will occur with increasing frequency. And sometimes, people will never know that they are communicating with a machine at all. In May 2018, Google introduced Google Duplex, "an AI System for Accomplishing Real-World Tasks Over the Phone."[52] Google's demonstration showed the AI assistant making a call to schedule an appointment at a hair salon.

Despite its usefulness, some people were upset. Unlike the robot speech of other systems, Google Duplex used natural "ums" and "hmms" that made it sound like a real person. People said it was morally wrong for a computer to trick people and make them think they were talking to a real person. In response, Google said that it would change Google Duplex to identify itself as a robot when making calls. Whether it's a robotic caller, a television personality, or someone else, the question of who is an actual person will become a major concern as AI continues to evolve.

Death

In an episode of *Black Mirror*, a British television series that explores near-future dystopias and science fiction that goes out of control, a woman tries to cope with the death of her boyfriend Ash after a car accident. She turns to a service that creates a digital avatar of her boyfriend by using the data from his social media posts and text messages. At first, she interacts with Ash through an instant messaging program, much like a chatbot. Then, by uploading photos and videos to the service, Ash gains a voice much like a personal assistant. Finally, Ash's digital persona is transferred to a physical android. I won't spoil the ending, but episodes of *Black Mirror* tend to be dark.

In an example of life imitating art, such life-preservation—or, perhaps, life-imitation—technologies are starting to appear. Eugenia Kuyda, the founder and CEO of an AI company, was building chatbots when she wondered if she could use her late friend's old emails and text messages to digitally bring him back to life. It only took 8,000 lines of his digital interactions to create a likeness his friends and family found both familiar and uncanny.

Other companies rely on people sitting for interviews before they die. When American actor Ed Asner passed away in 2021, mourners were invited to talk with an interactive display of the screen legend. His son remarked, "Nothing could prepare me for what I was going to witness when I saw it." He said it was like having his father there in the room with them and that people were "blown away" by it.[53]

One day, many years into the future, we may be able to make digital copies of our brains. Such copies wouldn't just be an ANN's interpretation of what we leave behind but an actual conscious entity. Until that time, we can turn to the enhanced memory preservation technologies being developed today to offer us digital comfort in times of spiritual loss.

Conclusion

The seeds of AI were born from our ancestors' dreams, but none of them could have imagined the AI that exists now. Science fiction writer Arthur C. Clarke once wrote, "Any sufficiently advanced technology is indistinguishable from magic." If we could travel in a time machine 100 years into the future, we would surely see things that seem like magic to us. Today we can only guess how AI will advance and change the world going forward. Perhaps we won't be able to recognize the world in even 10 or 20 years.

What will we consider "intelligent" in the future? What will the impact of AI be on society? Will today's moral issues regarding AI be resolved? As you've read, AI is not just about technology, but it's also about philosophy and social science. And the definition has evolved with the technology. So is it a tool to use, a weapon to fear, or a friendly companion to chat with? You now have the understanding to judge these questions for yourself.

In the introduction to this book, I encouraged you to view AI through the lens of an intelligent agent. An intelligent agent, if you remember, tries to accomplish certain goals by taking autonomous and rational actions based on how it perceives the world around it. Maybe while reading this book, you started to consider how you are an intelligent agent. The intelligence of your actions can be analyzed by evaluating how rational they are as you try to accomplish your goals.

To close out this book, let's ask our intelligent agent friend at OpenAI to help out with a short request, "Write the final paragraph in a book that describes the present state of AI.":

The state of AI is rapidly changing and evolving. With the advent of new technologies, AI is becoming more and more advanced. However, there are still many challenges that need to be addressed. For example, AI systems still have difficulty understanding and responding to natural language. They also often struggle to deal with complex tasks that require reasoning and problem solving. Nevertheless, AI is making great strides and is becoming increasingly powerful and sophisticated. In the future, AI will likely play an even more important role in our lives and the world.[54]

Endnotes

1 http://jmc.stanford.edu/artificial-intelligence/what-is-ai/index.html

2 https://en.wikipedia.org/wiki/Golem

3 https://en.wikipedia.org/wiki/R.U.R.

4 https://en.wikipedia.org/wiki/Markov_chain

5 Ganapathi, Padmavathi, and D. Shanmugapriya. Handbook of Research on Machine and Deep Learning Applications for Cyber Security. IGI Global, 2019.

6 https://www.computingreviews.com/todaysissue/todaysissue_quote.cfm?quote_id=366

7 https://bdtechtalks.com/2019/11/18/what-is-symbolic-artificial-intelligence/

8 https://www.nytimes.com/1958/07/08/archives/new-navy-device-learns-by-doing-psychologist-shows-embryo-of.html

9 https://cs.stanford.edu/people/eroberts/courses/soco/projects/neural-networks/History/history1.html

10 https://commons.wikimedia.org/wiki/File:Decision_Tree_vs._Random_Forest.png

11 https://99percentinvisible.org/episode/the-eliza-effect/transcript/

12 https://en.wikipedia.org/wiki/ELIZA

13 https://www.wired.com/2013/01/traveling-salesman-problem/

14 https://en.wikipedia.org/wiki/Nearest_neighbour_algorithm

15 https://en.wikipedia.org/wiki/Intelligent_agent

16 https://commons.wikimedia.org/wiki/File:Decision_Tree_vs._Random_Forest.png

17 https://en.wikipedia.org/wiki/Mechanical_Turk#/media/File:Racknitz_-_The_Turk_3.jpg

18 Russell, D. (2021). The BOXES methodology second edition: Black box control of ill-defined systems. New York: Springer.

19 https://cs.stanford.edu/people/eroberts/courses/soco/projects/1998-99/game-theory/Minimax.html

20 https://www.bbc.com/news/technology-50573071

21 https://www.newscientist.com/article/2119815-ai-just-won-a-poker-tournament-against-professional-players/

22 https://www.nytimes.com/2022/01/18/magazine/ai-technology-poker.html

23 Freedman, L. (2013). Strategy: A history. Oxford, UK: Oxford University Press.

24 https://www.japantimes.co.jp/news/2017/02/02/business/tech/artificial-intelligence-beats-humans-for-the-first-time-in-poker/, https://www.nytimes.

com/2022/01/18/magazine/ai-technology-poker.html

25 https://www.theguardian.com/technology/2019/oct/30/ai-becomes-grandmaster-in-fiendishly-complex-starcraft-ii

26 https://www.deepmind.com/blog/alphastar-mastering-the-real-time-strategy-game-starcraft-ii

27 https://www.nytimes.com/2021/07/16/technology/what-happened-ibm-watson.html

28 https://www.theatlantic.com/technology/archive/2021/09/i-weapons-are-third-revolution-warfare/620013/

29 https://www.bbc.com/news/technology-59810383

30 https://www.nist.gov/news-events/news/2022/03/theres-more-ai-bias-biased-data-nist-report-highlights

31 https://www.thoughtco.com/examples-of-institutional-racism-in-the-u-s-2834624

32 https://www.thoughtco.com/examples-of-institutional-racism-in-the-u-s-2834624

33 https://www.engadget.com/meta-unleashes-blender-bot-3-upon-the-internet-its-most-competent-chat-ai-to-date-150021062.html

34 https://www.mirror.co.uk/news/us-news/metas-ai-chatbot-turns-boss-27721493

35 https://www.vox.com/future-perfect/22916602/ai-bias-fairness-tradeoffs-artificial-intelligence

36 https://hbr.org/2022/01/where-automated-job-interviews-fall-short

37 https://www.bostonmagazine.com/news/2018/02/23/artificial-intelligence-race-dark-skin-bias/

38 https://www.scientificamerican.com/podcast/episode/beethovens-unfinished-10th-symphony-brought-to-life-by-artificial-intelligence/

39 https://www.scientificamerican.com/podcast/episode/beethovens-unfinished-10th-symphony-brought-to-life-by-artificial-intelligence/

40 https://www.vice.com/en/article/bvmvqm/an-ai-generated-artwork-won-first-place-at-a-state-fair-fine-arts-competition-and-artists-are-pissed?utm_source=reddit.com

41 https://arstechnica.com/information-technology/2022/09/flooded-with-ai-generated-images-some-art-communities-ban-them-completely/

42 https://www.pfizer.com/news/articles/how_a_novel_incubation_sandbox_helped_speed_up_data_analysis_in_pfizer_s_covid_19_vaccine_trial

43 https://www.sae.org/blog/sae-j3016-update

44 https://en.wikipedia.org/wiki/Trolley_problem

45 https://www.investopedia.com/terms/a/algorithmictrading.asp

46 https://www.ibm.com/blogs/watson/2021/06/equbot-aieq-ai-powered-etf/

47 https://www.ibm.com/blogs/watson/2021/06/equbot-aieq-ai-powered-etf/

48 https://www.deere.com/en/news/all-news/autonomous-tractor-reveal/

49 https://www.nytimes.com/2017/05/12/magazine/can-prairie-dogs-talk.html

50 https://www.nytimes.com/2022/08/30/science/translators-animals-naked-mole-rats.html

51 https://www.nytimes.com/2022/08/30/science/translators-animals-naked-mole-rats.html

52 https://ai.googleblog.com/2018/05/duplex-ai-system-for-natural-conversation.html

53 https://www.axios.com/2022/07/13/artificial-intelligence-chatbots-dead-relatives-grandma

54 https://beta.openai.com/playground

Word List

・本文で使われている全ての語を掲載しています（LEVEL 1、2）。ただし、LEVEL 3以上は、中学校レベルの語を含みません。

・語形が規則変化する語の見出しは原形で示しています。不規則変化語は本文中で使われている形になっています。

・一般的な意味を紹介していますので、一部の語で本文で実際に使われている品詞や意味と合っていないことがあります。

・品詞は以下のように示しています。

[名] 名詞	[代] 代名詞	[形] 形容詞	[副] 副詞	[動] 動詞	[助] 助動詞
[前] 前置詞	[接] 接続詞	[間] 間投詞	[冠] 冠詞	[略] 略語	[俗] 俗語
[頭] 接頭語	[尾] 接尾語	[号] 記号	[関] 関係代名詞		

A

☐ **ability** [名] ①できること，(～する) 能力 ②才能

☐ **about** [熟] **bring about** 引き起こす **come about** 起こる **go about one's daily business** 日々を送る，日常生活を続ける

☐ **absence** [名] 欠席，欠如，不在

☐ **absolutely** [副] ①完全に，確実に ②《yesを強調する返事として》そうですとも

☐ **abstract** [動] 抽出する，要約する

☐ **academia** [名] (大学などの) 学究的環境，学界

☐ **academic** [形] ①学校の，大学の ②学問の

☐ **academy** [名] ①アカデミー，学士院 ②学園，学院

☐ **acceleration** [名] 加速すること

☐ **accent** [名] アクセント，口調，特徴

☐ **accept** [動] ①受け入れる ②同意する，認める

☐ **access** [動] アクセスする

☐ **accessible** [形] 近づきやすい，利用できる

☐ **accident** [名] ①(不慮の) 事故，災難 ②偶然

☐ **accomplish** [動] 成し遂げる，果たす

☐ **according** [副]《– to ～》～によれば[よると]

☐ **accordingly** [副] ①それに応じて，適宜に ②従って，(～と) いうわけだから

☐ **account** [名] ①計算書 ②勘定，預金口座 ③説明，報告，記述 [動] ①《– for ～》～を説明する，～(の割合) を占める，～の原因となる ②～を…とみなす

☐ **accountable** [形] ①《– for ～》～に責任がある ②もっともな，無理もない

☐ **accounting** [名] 会計，経理

☐ **accuracy** [名] 正確さ，精度，的確さ

☐ **accurate** [形] ①正確な，間違いのない ②精密な

☐ **achievable** [形] 成し遂げられる，達成[成就] 可能な

☐ **achieve** [動] 成し遂げる，達成する，成功を収める

☐ **achievement** [名] ①達成，成就 ②業績

☐ **acquaintance** [名] ①知人，知り合い ②面識，知識

☐ **act** 動 ①行動する ②機能する ③演じる

☐ **activation** 名（ソフトウェアのライセンスなどの）有効化

☐ **activation function** 活性化関数《ニューラルネットワークのニューロンにおける，入力のなんらかの合計（しばしば，線形な重み付け総和）から，出力を決定するための関数で，非線形な関数とすることが多い》

☐ **activity** 名 活動，活気

☐ **actor** 名 俳優，役者

☐ **actual** 形 実際の，現実の

☐ **actually** 副 実際に，本当に，実は

☐ **Ada Lovelace** エイダ・ラブレース《19世紀のイギリスの貴族・数学者。初期の汎用計算機である解析機関についての著作で，世界初のコンピュータープログラマーとして知られる1815-1852》

☐ **adapt** 動 ①適応する［させる］ ②脚色する，編曲する，翻案する

☐ **adaptive** 形 適応［順応］できる

☐ **ADAS** 略 先進運転支援システム《自動車のドライバーの運転操作を支援するシステム。advanced driver assist system の略》

☐ **add** 動 ①加える，足す ②足し算をする ③言い添える

☐ **addition** 名 ①付加，追加，添加 ②足し算 **in addition** 加えて，さらに

☐ **additional** 形 追加の，さらなる

☐ **address** 動 ①あて名を書く ②演説をする，話しかける

☐ **adjust** 動 ①適応する［させる］，慣れる ②調整する ③（意見の食い違い・論争などを）解決する，調停する ④（間違いなどを）訂正する

☐ **admission** 名 ①入場（許可），入会，入学，入社 ②入場料

☐ **advance** 名 進歩，前進

☐ **advanced** 形 上級の，先に進んだ，高等の

☐ **advanced driver assist system (ADAS)** 先進運転支援システム《自動車のドライバーの運転操作を支援するシステム》

☐ **advantage** 名 有利な点［立場］，強み，優越 **take advantage of** ～を利用する，～につけ込む

☐ **advent** 名 ①《the －》到来，出現 ②《A-》キリストの降臨，降臨節

☐ **advertising** 名 広告，宣伝

☐ **advisor** 名 忠告者，助言者，顧問

☐ **affect** 動 ①影響する ②（病気などが）おかす ③ふりをする

☐ **after** 熟 **after all** やはり，結局 **after that** その後 **come after** ～のあとを追う

☐ **agent** 名 ①代理人 ②代表者 **intelligent agent** 知的エージェント《一種の人工知能的機能を有するソフトウェアエージェント。ユーザーを補助し，繰り返し行うべきコンピューター関連のタスクをユーザーに代わって行うエージェントで，学習し「適応」する能力を有する》 **rational agent** 合理的エージェント《エージェントが置かれている，環境で最良の結果を達成するために行動するエージェント》

☐ **Agent Smith** エージェント・スミス《アメリカのSFアクション映画『マトリックス』の登場人物》

☐ **aggregation** 名 集合，集成

☐ **aggregation bias** 集計バイアス《集計されたデータに見られる傾向が個々のデータポイントにも適用されると誤って仮定された場合に発生する》

☐ **AGI** 略 汎用人工知能《「人間と同様の感性や思考回路をもつ」人工知能のことを指す。artificial general intelligence の略》

☐ **agility** 名 機敏，敏捷さ

☐ **agree with** （人）に同意する

☐ **agriculture** 名 農業，農耕

☐ **ahead of** ～より先［前］に

A B C D E F G H I J K L M N O P Q R S T U V W X Y Z

□ **Ahmed Elgammal** アーメド・エルガマル《ラトガース大学コンピューターサイエンス学部教授。AIが人間の介入なしに創造的になれるかどうかを探求する先駆的な研究を行っている》

□ **AI** 略 人工知能《Artificial intelligenceの略》 **connectionist AI** コネクショニストAI《一般的には，ニューラルネットワーク型ＡＩを指す》 **deep AI** ディープAI《強いAI（strong AI）の言い換え》 **narrow AI** 弱いAI《人間の知能の一部に特化した機能を実現するAIのこと。特化型AIも似たような意味で使われる。weak AIと同義》 **strong AI** 強いAI《人類よりも優れた推論能力を持つAI（人工知能）のこと》 **symbolic AI** シンボリックAI《1950年代に遡る，第１次AIブームで支配的だったパラダイムで，知識を記号で表現し，問題を解くために推論など，記号上の計算を行う》 **weak AI** 弱いAI《人間の知能の一部に特化した機能を実現するAIのこと。特化型AIも似たような意味で使われる。narrow AIと同義》

□ **AI Effect** AI効果

□ **AI winter** AIの冬，AI冬の時代

□ **AI-based** 形 AIベースの

□ **aid** 名 援助（者），助け

□ **AI-enabled** 形 AI対応の

□ **AIEQ** 略 AIEQ《AIが運用する上場投資信託（ETF）。AI Powered Equity ETFの略》

□ **AI-generated** 形 AIによって生み出される

□ **AI-powered** 形 AI式の，AIで動作する

□ **Ajeeb** 名 アジーブ《チャールズ・フーパー（家具職人）が製作したチェスをする自動人形》

□ **Alan Turing** アラン・チューリング《イギリスの数学者，暗号研究者，計算機科学者，哲学者。電子計算機の黎明期の研究に従事し，情報処理の基礎的・原理的分野において大きな貢献をした。1912-1954》

□ **Alaska** 名 アラスカ州

□ **Alberta** 名 アルバータ州《カナダ》

□ **alert** 名 警報，警戒 **spoiler alert** ネタバレ注意

□ **Alex Bernstein** アレックス・バーンスタイン《アメリカの数学者，チェスプレイヤー，コンピューターチェスのパイオニア。1930-1999》

□ **Alexa** 名 アレクサ《Amazonが開発したバーチャルアシスタントAI技術。音声対話，音楽再生，ToDoリストの作成，アラームの設定，ポッドキャストのストリーミング，オーディオブックの再生，天気，交通，スポーツ，その他ニュースなどのリアルタイム情報の提供が可能》

□ **Alexander Pushkin** アレクサンドル・プーシキン《ロシアの詩人・作家。ロシア近代文学の嚆矢とされる。1799-1837》

□ **algorithm** 名 アルゴリズム《数学的な問題を解くための一連の手順》 **nearest neighbor algorithm** 最近傍法《ニアレストネイバー法ともいう。 新しいデータに対し，もっとも近い（数個の）既存データが属するクラスター（集団）に分類する》

□ **algorithm bias** アルゴリズムバイアス《偏った学習データを与えてしまったことにより，機械学習のアルゴリズムが偏った結果を学習してしまうこと》

□ **algorithmic** 形 アルゴリズムの［に関する］

□ **algorithmic trading** アルゴリズム取引《一度に処理しきれないほどの大口の注文を，プログラムによる自動取引により，時間・価格・出来高に基づき，より小さな注文に分割して発注する取引方法の事。投資銀行や年金基金や投資信託会社やヘッジファンドで広く利用されている》

□ **alike** 形 よく似ている

□ **Alison Barker** アリソン・バーカー《マックス・プランク脳研究所の神

経科学者》

☐ **all** 熟 **after all** やはり，結局 **all over the world** 世界中に **all the way** ずっと **at all** 一体 **for all ~** ~にもかかわらず **not ~ at all** 少しも[全然]~ない

☐ **Allen Newell** アレン・ニューウェル《初期の人工知能研究の研究者。1975年，人工知能と認知心理学への基礎的貢献が認められ，ハーバート・サイモンと共にACMチューリング賞を受賞。1927-1992》

☐ **allow** 動 ①許す，《– … to ~》…が~するのを可能にする，…に~させておく ②与える

☐ **all-women's college** 女子大

☐ **ally** 動 同盟する，連合する 名 同盟国，味方

☐ **along with** ~と一緒に

☐ **Alphabet** 名 アルファベット《2015年にGoogle Inc.（現・Google LLC）およびグループ企業の持株会社として設立された，アメリカ合衆国の多国籍テクノロジー・コングロマリット》

☐ **alphabetically** 副 アルファベット順に

☐ **AlphaFold** 名 アルファフォールド《タンパク質の構造予測を実行するGoogleのDeepMindによって開発された人工知能プログラム》

☐ **AlphaGo** 名 アルファ碁《Google DeepMind社によって開発されたコンピューター囲碁プログラム。2015年10月に，人間のプロ囲碁棋士を互先（ハンディキャップなし）で破った初のコンピューター囲碁プログラムとなった》

☐ **AlphaStar** 名 アルファスター《DeepMindが開発した，リアルタイム戦略ゲーム「スタークラフト2」の対戦AI》

☐ **AlphaZero** 名 アルファゼロ《DeepMindによって開発されたコンピュータープログラム。AlphaGo Zero（AGZ）アルゴリズムのより汎化された変種であり，囲碁とともに将棋とチェスがプレーできる》

☐ **alternate** 動 交替する，交互に起こる

☐ **although** 接 ~だけれども，~にもかかわらず，たとえ~でも

☐ **altogether** 副 まったく，全然，全部で

☐ **amateur** 形 しろうとの，道楽の

☐ **amazing** 形 驚くべき，見事な

☐ **Amazon** 名 アマゾン《Amazon.com》

☐ **American** 形 アメリカ（人）の 名 アメリカ人

☐ **amount** 名 ①量，額 ②《the –》合計

☐ **analogy** 名 ①類似（点） ②類推

☐ **analysis** 名 分析，解析（学）

☐ **analyst** 名 専門家，分析家，解説者

☐ **analytics** 名 分析

☐ **analyze** 動 ①分析する，解析する，細かく検討する ②精神分析する ③解剖する

☐ **ancestor** 名 ①祖先，先祖 ②先人

☐ **ancient** 形 昔の，古代の

☐ **Andrey Markov** アンドレイ・マルコフ《ロシアの数学者。特に確率過程論に関する業績で知られ，彼の研究成果は，後にマルコフ連鎖として知られるようになった。1856-1922》

☐ **android** 名 アンドロイド，人造人間

☐ **ANI** 略 特化型AI《特定のタスク（処理）のみを実現するAI。artificial narrow intelligenceの略》

☐ **animal** 熟 **animal behavior** 動物行動学

☐ **animate** 動 生気[元気]を与える

☐ **ANN** 略 人工ニューラルネットワーク《人間の脳内にある神経細胞（ニューロン）の動作を模したコンピューティングシステム。artificial neural

A B C D E F G H I J K L M N O P Q R S T U V W X Y Z

networkの略》

□ **announce** 動（人に）知らせる，公表する

□ **anonymized** 形 匿名化された

□ **anonymous** 形 作者不明の，匿名の

□ **another** 熟 **one another** お互い **yet another** さらにもう一つの

□ **anymore** 副《通例否定文，疑問文で》今はもう，これ以上，これから

□ **anyone** 代 ①《疑問文・条件節で》誰か ②《否定文で》誰も（～ない） ③《肯定文で》誰でも

□ **anyway** 副 ①いずれにせよ，ともかく ②どんな方法でも

□ **apart** 副 ①ばらばらに，離れて ②別にして，それだけで

□ **app** 名 アプリ

□ **appeal** 動 ①求める，訴える ②（人の）気に入る

□ **appear** 動 ①現れる，見えてくる ②（～のように）見える，～らしい **appear to** するように見える

□ **applicant** 名 応募者，志願者

□ **application** 名 ①申し込み，応募，申し込み書 ②適用，応用

□ **apply** 動 ①申し込む，志願する ②あてはまる ③適用する

□ **appointment** 名 ①（会合などの）約束，予約 ②任命，指名

□ **appreciation** 名 ①正しい評価，真価を認めること ②感謝

□ **approach** 名 接近，（～へ）近づく道

□ **appropriate** 形 ①適切な，ふさわしい，妥当な ②特殊な，特有の

□ **approximate** 形 おおよその，近似の

□ **approximately** 副 おおよそ，だいたい

□ **approximation** 名 概算，見積もり，近似値

□ **arbitrary** 形 ①気ままな，勝手な ②任意の

□ **architecture** 名 ①建築（学），建築物（様式） ②構成，構造

□ **argue** 動 ①論じる，議論する ②主張する

□ **argument** 名 ①議論，論争 ②論拠，理由

□ **army** 名 軍隊，《the －》陸軍

□ **around** 熟 **around the clock** 24時間ぶっ通しで **around the corner** すぐ近くに **go around** 広まる，まん延する **walk around** 歩き回る，ぶらぶら歩く

□ **arrange** 動 ①並べる，整える ②取り決める ③準備する，手はずを整える

□ **arrangement** 名 ①準備，手配 ②取り決め，協定 ③整頓，配置

□ **arrival** 名 ①到着 ②到達

□ **Arthur C. Clarke** アーサー・C・クラーク《イギリス出身のSF作家。20世紀を代表するSF作家の一人。1917-2008》

□ **Arthur Samuel** アーサー・サミュエル《アメリカの計算機科学者で，コンピューターゲームと人工知能の分野で主に知られている。1901-1990》

□ **article** 名 ①（法令・誓約などの）箇条，項目 ②（新聞・雑誌などの）記事，論文

□ **artificial** 形 ①人工的な ②不自然な，わざとらしい

□ **artificial general intelligence (AGI)** 汎用人工知能《「人間と同様の感性や思考回路をもつ」人工知能のことを指す》

□ **artificial intelligence (AI)** 人工知能

□ **Artificial Intelligence: A Modern Approach** 『人工知能：現代のアプローチ』《スチュアート・J・ラッセルとピーター・ノーヴィグによって書かれた人工知能に関する大学

の教科書》

□ **artificial neural network (ANN)** 人工ニューラルネットワーク《人間の脳内にある神経細胞（ニューロン）の動作を模したコンピューティングシステム》

□ **artificial narrow intelligence (ANI)** 特化型AI《特定のタスク（処理）のみを実現するAI》

□ **artificial super intelligence (ASI)** 人工超知能《人間をはるかに上回る知性を獲得した人工知能として仮定されているもの》

□ **artificially** 副 人為的に，人工的に，見かけ上は

□ **artist** 名 芸術家

□ **artistic** 形 芸術的な，芸術（家）の

□ **artistry** 名 芸術性

□ **artwork** 名 アートワーク，芸術作品

□ **as** 熟 **as a whole** 全体として **as for** ～に関しては，～はどうかと言うと **as if** あたかも～のように，まるで～みたいに **as much as** ～と同じだけ **as to** ～に関しては，～に応じて **as well** なお，その上，同様に **as well as** ～と同様に **be known as** ～として知られている **so as to** ～するように，～するために **such as** たとえば～，～のような **such ～ as** ……のような～ **the same ～ as** ……と同じ（ような）～

□ **Ash** 名 アッシュ《『ブラック・ミラー』の登場人物》

□ **ASI** 略 人工超知能《人間をはるかに上回る知性を獲得した人工知能として仮定されているもの。artificial super intelligenceの略》

□ **Asian** 形 アジア人の

□ **aside** 副 わきへ（に），離れて **aside from** ～はさておき

□ **assemble** 動 ①集める，集まる ②組み立てる

□ **asset** 名 財産，資産，価値のあるもの

□ **assign** 動 任命する，割り当てる

□ **assist** 動 手伝う，列席する，援助する

□ **assistance** 名 援助，支援

□ **assistant** 名 助手，補佐，店員 **digital assistant** デジタル・アシスタント《通常はインターネットを介して，利用者との会話をシミュレートする高度なコンピューター・プログラム》 **virtual personal assistant** 仮想パーソナルアシスタント《個人のタスクまたはサービスを実行できるソフトウェアエージェント》

□ **associate** 動 ①連合［共同］する，提携する ②～を連想する

□ **association** 名 ①交際，連合，結合 ②連想 ③協会，組合

□ **assume** 動 ①仮定する，当然のことと思う ②引き受ける

□ **assumption** 名 前提，想定，仮定

□ **assured** 形 保証された，確実な

□ **at** 熟 **at a time** 一度に，続けざまに **at all** 一体 **at first** 最初は，初めのうちは **at least** 少なくとも **at the end of** ～の終わりに **at the time** そのころ，当時は **at work** 働いて，仕事中で，（機械が）稼動中で

□ **athlete** 名 運動選手

□ **atmosphere** 名 ①大気，空気 ②雰囲気

□ **attack** 動 ①襲う，攻める ②非難する ③（病気が）おかす

□ **attain** 動 達成する，成し遂げる，達する

□ **attainment** 名 ①到達，達成 ②《-s》（達成して得た）学識

□ **attempt** 動 試みる，企てる 名 試み，企て，努力

□ **attend** 動 ①出席する ②世話をする，仕える ③伴う ④《－to ～》～に注意を払う，専念する，～の世話をする

□ **attendee** 名（会議などの）出席者

□ **attention** 名 ①注意, 集中 ②配慮, 手当て, 世話

□ **attract** 動 ①引きつける, 引く ②魅力がある, 魅了する

□ **attribute** 名 特性, 属性

□ **audio** 名 オーディオ, 音声部

□ **Australia** 名 オーストラリア《国名》

□ **Austria** 名 オーストリア《国名》

□ **author** 名 著者, 作家

□ **automate** 動 自動化する

□ **automated** 形 オートメーション化された

□ **automated video interview (AVI)** 自動ビデオ面接《機械学習アルゴリズムを用いて面接者の性格特性や社会的スキルを予測するもので, 産業界で利用が拡大している》

□ **automatic** 形 自動の, オートマチックの

□ **automatically** 副 無意識に, 自動的に, 惰性的に

□ **automation** 名 オートメーション, 自動化

□ **automaton** 名 自動装置, 自動人形, ロボット, 機械的に行動する人

□ **automotive** 形 ①自動車の ②自動推進の

□ **autonomous** 形 自立した, 自律性の

□ **autonomy** 名 自律(性), 自主(性)

□ **available** 形 利用[使用・入手]できる, 得られる

□ **avatar** 名 アバター, 化身《インターネットなどの仮想空間における, 人間を具現化した3次元の動くイメージ》

□ **AVI** 略 自動ビデオ面接《機械学習アルゴリズムを用いて面接者の性格特性や社会的スキルを予測するもので, 産業界で利用が拡大している。automated video interviewの略》

□ **avoid** 動 避ける, (～を)しないようにする

□ **avoidable** 形 回避できる

□ **aware** 形 ①気がついて, 知って ②(～の)認識のある

□ **awareness** 名 認識, 自覚, 意識性, 気づいていること

□ **away** 熟 **blow away** 吹き払う, 吹き飛ばす, 立ち去る **pass away** 過ぎ去る, 終わる, 死ぬ **take away** ①連れ去る ②取り上げる, 奪い去る ③取り除く

□ **awful** 形 ①ひどい, 不愉快な ②恐ろしい

□ **axion** 名 アキシオン, 脳脊髄軸

B

□ **back** 熟 **back to life** 生き返る, 息を吹き返す **bring back** 戻す, 呼び戻す, 持ち帰る **fall back** 後退する, 戻る **get back** 戻る, 帰る **go back to** ～に帰る[戻る], ～に遡る, (中断していた作業に)再び取り掛かる

□ **backpropagation** 名 誤差逆伝播法《ネットワークの出力と正解ラベルとの誤差から, 各ニューロンのパラメータを修正する》

□ **backward** 副 後方へ, 逆に, 後ろ向きに

□ **bake** 動 (パンなどを)焼く

□ **balance** 動 釣り合いをとる

□ **ban** 名 禁止, 禁制

□ **bark** 名 ①ほえる声, どなり声 ②木の皮 動 ほえる, どなる

□ **Barry Cooper** バリー・クーパー《イギリスの作曲家・オルガニスト・音楽学者。ベートーヴェンの遺作《交響曲第10番》の実用譜を「完成」させた》

□ **base** 名 基礎, 土台, 本部 動《-on ～》～に基礎を置く, 基づく

□ **based on** 《be -》～に基づく

□ **basic** 形 基礎の，基本の

□ **battlefield** 名 戦場

□ **bead** 数珠玉，《-s》ビーズ［のネックレス］

□ **bear** 熟 **have no bearing on** ～に何の関係もない

□ **beat** 動 ①打つ，鼓動する ②打ち負かす

□ **beaten** 動 beat（打つ）の過去分詞

□ **because of** ～のために，～の理由で

□ **bed** 熟 **test bed** テストベッド《新技術の実証試験に使用されるプラットフォーム》

□ **beg** 動 懇願する，お願いする

□ **begin with** ～で始まる

□ **beginning** 動 begin（始まる）の現在分詞 名 初め，始まり

□ **behavior** 名 振る舞い，態度，行動 **animal behavior** 動物行動学

□ **behind** 前 ①～の後ろに，～の背後に ②～に遅れて，～に劣って 副 ①後ろに，背後に ②遅れて，劣って **leave behind** あとにする，～を置き去りにする

□ **benchmark** 名 水準点，基準，ベンチマーク

□ **benefit** 名 利益，恩恵

□ **Benjamin Franklin** ベンジャミン・フランクリン《アメリカ合衆国の政治家，外交官，著述家，物理学者，気象学者。1706-1790》

□ **Bent Larsen** ベント・ラーセン《デンマークのチェスプレーヤー。1935-2010》

□ **Berkeley** 名 バークレー《地名》

□ **best-selling** 形 ベストセラーの

□ **beta** 名 ベータ版

□ **beyond** 前 ～を越えて，～の向こうに 副 向こうに

□ **bias** 名 偏見，先入見，バイアス **aggregation bias** 集計バイアス《集計されたデータに見られる傾向が個々のデータポイントにも適用されると誤って仮定された場合に発生する》 **algorithm bias** アルゴリズムバイアス《偏った学習データを与えてしまったことにより，機械学習のアルゴリズムが偏った結果を学習してしまうこと》 **cognitive bias** 認知バイアス《物事の判断が，直感やこれまでの経験にもとづく先入観によって非合理的になる心理現象のこと》 **confirmation bias** 確証バイアス《仮説や信念を検証する際にそれを支持する情報ばかりを集め，反証する情報を無視または集めようとしない傾向のこと》 **exclusion bias** 除外バイアス《調査対象から特定の年齢層や人種・民族を除外する，あるいはデータが入手しやすいとの理由のみで調査対象を選出することによって生じる偏り》 **historical bias** 歴史的なバイアス《使用したデータが，もはや現在の現実を正確に反映していない場合に発生する》 **label bias** ラベルバイアス《局所的に見て連接しやすいラベルを正解として選択しやすく，結果的に全体でみると不自然な系列を選択してしまう現象》 **measurement bias** 測定バイアス《調査すべき変数に関して，対象者を不正確に測定（または分類）することによる系統的な誤差》 **prejudice bias** 偏見 **sample bias** サンプリングバイアス《不適切な標本抽出によって，母集団を代表しない特定の性質のデータが紛れ込んでいること》 **statistical bias** 統計的偏り，biasやバイアスの同義語 **systemic bias** 系統的バイアス《統計的な測定に，外部の圧力が影響を与えること》 動 偏見をもたせる

□ **big data** ビッグデータ《人間では全体を把握することが困難な巨大なデータ群のこと》

□ **big-picture** 形 大局的見地から見た

□ **billion** 形 10億の，ばく大な，無数の 名 10億

□ **billion-dollar** 形 10億ドルの

□ **binary** 形 2値の，2進法の

□ **biological** 形 ①生物学(上)の，生物学的な ②血のつながった

□ **biology** 名 生物学 **conservation biology** 保全生態学

□ **biomarker** 名 バイオマーカー《ある疾患の有無や，進行状態を示す目安となる生理学的指標のこと》

□ **biometric** 形 生体認証による

□ **birth** 名 ①出産，誕生 ②生まれ，起源，(よい)家柄

□ **black box** (複雑で仕組みが分からない)ブラック・ボックス

□ **Black Mirror** 『ブラック・ミラー』《英国のテレビドラマシリーズ。新しいテクノロジーがもたらす予期せぬ社会変化を描く，ダークで風刺的なSFアンソロジー》

□ **Blake Lemoine** ブレイク・ルモワン《Googleの元エンジニア。AIチャットシステム「LaMDA」が意識を持っていると主張して停職処分になり，その後解雇された》

□ **blame** 動 とがめる，非難する

□ **BlenderBot 3** BlenderBot 3《米Metaの AI部門Meta AIが公開したオンラインチャットボット。Tayを失敗に導いたトラブルと同じ類のものを回避するように設計されている》

□ **blog** 名 ブログ

□ **blood** 名 ①血，血液 ②血統，家柄 ③気質

□ **blow away** 吹き払う，吹き飛ばす，立ち去る

□ **blown** 動 blow(吹く)の過去分詞

□ **bluff** 動 はったりを言う

□ **bluffing** 名 空威張り

□ **board** 名 板，掲示板

□ **board game** ボードゲーム

□ **bond** 名 債券，公債，社債

□ **boss** 名 上司，親方，監督

□ **bot** 名 ボット《人間の補助をするソフトウェア・エージェント》

□ **bound** 名 境界(線)，限界 **by leaps and bounds** (進行・成長などが)急速に，飛躍的に

□ **boyfriend** 名 男友だち

□ **brain** 名 ①脳 ②知力

□ **brake** 名 ブレーキ，歯止め

□ **braking** 名 制動 **phantom braking** ファントムブレーキ《主にオートパイロット使用時に見られる誤認緊急停止。なんの前触れもなく勝手に自動で緊急ブレーキがかかること》

□ **branch** 名 ①枝 ②支流，支部

□ **breadth** 名 幅，横幅

□ **breakthrough** 名 突破，打開，ブレークスルー

□ **brief** 形 ①短い時間の ②簡単な

□ **bring about** 引き起こす

□ **bring back** 戻す，呼び戻す，持ち帰る

□ **British** 形 ①英国人の ②イギリス英語の 名 英国人

□ **brittle** 形 もろい，砕けやすい

□ **broad** 形 ①幅の広い ②寛大な ③明白な

□ **broadly** 副 大ざっぱに，露骨に

□ **Broadway** 名 (劇場の)ブロードウェイ

□ **bronze** 名 ブロンズ，青銅

□ **bug** 名 ①小虫 ②細菌，ウイルス ③(ソフト・プログラムの)バグ 動 (～を)困らせる，イライラさせる

□ **burrow** 名 (小動物(ウサギやキツネ)の)巣穴，隠れ穴

□ **Bush** 名 ジョージ・W・ブッシュ《第43代米国大統領，1946–》

□ **business** 熟 **go about one's daily business** 日々を送る，日常生活を続ける

□ **but** 熟 **not only ～ but (also) …** ～だけでなく…もまた **not ～ but …**

〜ではなくて…

□ **by** 熟 **by leaps and bounds** (進行・成長などが) 急速に, 飛躍的に **by means of** 〜を用いて **by oneself** 一人で, 自分だけで, 独力で **by the time** 〜する時までに **one by one** 1つずつ, 1人ずつ **pass by** 〜のそばを通る [通り過ぎる]

C

□ **C-3PO** 名 シースリーピーオー《アメリカのSF映画『スター・ウォーズ』シリーズの登場人物 (ロボット/ドロイド)》

□ **cabinet** 名 ①飾り棚 ②《C-》内閣, 閣僚

□ **calculate** 動 ①計算する, 算出する ②見積もる, 予想する

□ **calculation** 名 計算, 勘定, 見積もり

□ **California** 名 カリフォルニア《米国の州》

□ **caller** 名 訪問者, 電話をかける人

□ **camera** 名 カメラ **stereo camera** ステレオカメラ《対象物を複数の異なる方向から同時に撮影することにより, その奥行き方向の情報も記録できるようにしたカメラ》

□ **campaign** 名 ①キャンペーン (活動, 運動) ②政治運動, 選挙運動 ③軍事行動

□ **campus** 名 キャンパス, (大学などの) 構内

□ **Canadian** 形 カナダ (人) の 名 カナダ人

□ **candidate** 名 ①立候補者 ②学位取得希望者 ③志願者

□ **capability** 名 ①能力, 才能 ②機能, 性能 ③可能性, 将来性

□ **capable** 形 ①《be – of 〜 [〜ing]》〜の能力 [資質] がある ②有能な

□ **capacity** 名 ①定員, 容量 ②能力, (潜在的な) 可能性

□ **captain** 名 長, 船長, 首領, 主将

□ **capture** 動 捕える

□ **care** 熟 **health care** 健康保険制度 **take care of** 〜の世話をする, 〜の面倒を見る, 〜を管理する

□ **Carl Rogers** カール・ロジャーズ《アメリカ合衆国の臨床心理学者。来談者中心療法 (Client-Centered Therapy) を創始した。1902-1987》

□ **Carnegie Mellon University (CMU)** カーネギーメロン大学

□ **carry on** ①続ける ②持ち運ぶ

□ **carry out** [計画を] 実行する

□ **case** 熟 **edge case** エッジケース《極端な動作パラメータでのみ発生する問題または状況》 **in the case of** 〜の場合は

□ **cash** 名 現金 (払い)

□ **category** 名 カテゴリー, 種類, 部類

□ **celebrity** 名 ①有名人, 名士 ②名声

□ **cell** 名 ①細胞 ②小区分, 小室, 独房

□ **CEO** 略 最高経営責任者 (= Chief Executive Officer)

□ **certain** 形 ①確実な, 必ず〜する ②(人が) 確信した ③ある ④いくらかの

□ **certainly** 副 ①確かに, 必ず ②《返答に用いて》もちろん, そのとおり, 承知しました

□ **certainty** 名 確信, 確実性

□ **challenge** 名 ①挑戦 ②難関 **penny challenge** ペニーチャレンジ《コンセントに充電器のプラグを半分ほど挿した状態でプラグに硬貨を落下させるというもの。硬貨が充電器のプラグに接触すると大電流が流れ, 火花が出る》

□ **challenger** 名 挑戦者

□ **champion** 名 優勝者, チャンピオン

A B C D E F G H I J K L M N O P Q R S T U V W X Y Z

□ **championship** 名 選手権(試合)

□ **chance** 熟 **not stand a chance** まるで歯が立たない

□ **chapter** 名 (書物の)章

□ **character** 名 ①特性, 個性 ②(小説・劇などの)登場人物 ③文字, 記号 ④品性, 人格

□ **characteristic** 名 特徴, 特性, 特色, 持ち味

□ **charger** 名 充電器

□ **charm** 動 魅了する

□ **chat** 動 おしゃべりをする, 談笑する

□ **chatbot** 名 チャットボット《「チャット」と「ボット」を組み合わせた言葉で, 自動的に会話を行うプログラムのこと》

□ **check** 動 ①照合する, 検査する ②阻止[妨害]する ③(所持品を)預ける 名 ①照合, 検査 ②小切手 ③(突然の)停止, 阻止(するもの) ④伝票, 勘定書 **keep ~ in check** ~を抑制[制止・阻止・防止・けん制]する

□ **checker** 名 チェック係, チェックする人

□ **checkers** 名 チェッカー《2人で互いの12個の黒と赤のコマを取り合うボード・ゲーム》

□ **checkmate** 名《チェス》チェックメイト, 王手詰み

□ **checkup** 名 ①(機械などの)点検 ②健康診断

□ **cheese** 名 チーズ

□ **chess** 名 チェス《西洋将棋》

□ **chessboard** 名 チェス盤, 戦局

□ **chess-playing** 形 チェスをプレイする

□ **chest** 名 胸, 肺

□ **chief** 形 最高位の, 第一の, 主要な

□ **Chief Investment Officer** 最高投資責任者

□ **China** 名 ①中国《国名》②《c-》陶磁器, 瀬戸物

□ **Chinese** 形 中国(人)の 名 ①中国人 ②中国語

□ **chirp** 名 (小鳥・虫の)ちいちい鳴く声

□ **choice** 名 選択(の範囲・自由), えり好み, 選ばれた人[物]

□ **Chris Natividad** クリス・ナティヴィダド《エクボット社のCIO兼共同設立者》

□ **Chris Watkins** クリス・ワトキンズ《ロイヤルホロウェイ大学コンピューターサイエンス学部教授。「Q学習」(Q-learning)という名前で近年流行りの機械学習の手法をまとめた》

□ **cilia** 名《動物》(細胞の)繊毛《cilium の複数形》

□ **circuit** 名 ①1周, 巡回 ②回路 ③サーキット, レース場

□ **circumstance** 名 ①(周囲の)事情, 状況, 環境 ②《-s》(人の)境遇, 生活状態

□ **citizen** 名 ①市民, 国民 ②住民, 民間人

□ **claim** 動 ①主張する ②要求する, 請求する

□ **classical** 形 古典の, クラシックの

□ **classification** 名 分類, 等級, 区分

□ **classification model** 分類モデル《あるデータがどのクラスに属すかを判別するモデル》

□ **classify** 動 分類する, 区別する

□ **clay** 名 粘土, 白土

□ **clear** 形 ①はっきりした, 明白な ②澄んだ ③(よく)晴れた 動 ①はっきりさせる ②片づける ③晴れる

□ **clever** 形 ①頭のよい, 利口な ②器用な, 上手な

□ **client** 名 依頼人, 顧客, クライアント

□ **Clifford Shaw** クリフォード・ショー《アメリカ合衆国のシステム・プ

ログラマ。世界初の人工知能プログラムとされるLogic Theoristの共同開発者のひとりであり，1950年代のプログラミング言語であるInformation Processing Language（IPL）の開発者のひとりである。1922-1991》

□ **climate** 名気候，風土，環境

□ **clinical** 形 ①臨床の，臨床治療の ②客観的な態度の，冷静な

□ **clock** 熟 **around the clock** 24時間ぶっ通しで

□ **closely** 副 ①密接に ②念入りに，詳しく ③ぴったりと

□ **clustering** 名クラスタリング《教師なし学習の一種で，データ間の類似度にもとづいて，データをグループ分けする手法》

□ **CMU** 略カーネギーメロン大学《Carnegie Mellon Universityの略》

□ **CNN** 略畳み込みニューラルネットワーク《層間を共通重みの局所結合で繋いだニューラルネットワークの総称・クラス。機械学習，特に画像や動画認識に広く使われる。convolutional neural networkの略》

□ **co-author** 動共同で執筆する

□ **code** 名コード，プログラム

□ **Codex** 名コーデックス《自然言語に基づいたコーディングアシスタントAI》

□ **coding** 名コーディング，プログラミング

□ **co-founder** 名共同創立者

□ **cognitive** 名認識［認知］力［作用］の

□ **cognitive bias** 認知バイアス《物事の判断が，直感やこれまでの経験にもとづく先入観によって非合理的になる心理現象のこと》

□ **coin** 動（新しい言葉を）作る

□ **collaborator** 名協力者，共同制作者

□ **collection** 名収集，収蔵物

□ **collision** 名衝突，不一致，あつれき

□ **colloquial** 形話し言葉の，口語の

□ **colony** 名植民［移民］（地）

□ **Colorado State Fair** コロラドステートフェア《コロラド州プエブロで毎年8月下旬に開催されるイベント》

□ **colored** 形 ①色のついた ②有色人種の，黒人の

□ **Columbia University** コロンビア大学

□ **combination** 名 ①結合（状態，行為），団結 ②連合，同盟

□ **combine** 動 ①結合する［させる］②連合する，協力する

□ **come about** 起こる

□ **come after** ～のあとを追う

□ **come into** ～に入ってくる

□ **come up with** ～に追いつく，～を思いつく，考え出す，見つけ出す

□ **comedian** 名喜劇役者，コメディアン

□ **comfort** 名 ①快適さ，満足 ②慰め ③安楽

□ **commercially** 副商業的に

□ **common** 熟 **in common** 共通して

□ **commonly** 副一般に，通例

□ **communicate** 動 ①知らせる，連絡する ②理解し合う

□ **communication** 名伝えること，伝導，連絡

□ **community** 名 ①団体，共同社会，地域社会 ②《the –》社会（一般），世間 ③共有，共同責任

□ **companion** 名 ①友，仲間，連れ ②添えもの，つきもの

□ **comparable** 形比較できる，匹敵する

□ **compare** 動 ①比較する，対照する ②たとえる

□ **comparison** 名比較, 対照

□ **compete** 動①競争する ②(競技に)参加する ③匹敵する

□ **competition** 名競争, 競合, コンペ

□ **competitive** 形競争の, 競争心の強い, (品質などが)他に負けない

□ **complain** 動①不平[苦情]を言う, ぶつぶつ言う ②(病状などを)訴える

□ **complete** 形完全な, まったくの, 完成した 動完成させる

□ **completely** 副完全に, すっかり

□ **complex** 形入り組んだ, 複雑な, 複合の

□ **complicated** 形①複雑な ②むずかしい, 困難な

□ **component** 名構成要素, 部品, 成分

□ **composer** 名作曲家, 作者

□ **computation** 名計算, 評価, 計算結果

□ **compute** 動計算する

□ **computer-generated** 形コンピューターで作った, コンピューター処理の

□ **computing** 形コンピューターの

□ **Computing Machinery and Intelligence** 「計算する機械と知性」《1950年10月,「Mind」誌で発表された論文。人工知能の問題を提起, 今日チューリングテストとして知られている実験を提案している》

□ **computing power** 計算[演算・計算]能力

□ **Con Slobodchikoff** コン・スロボドチコフ《動物行動学者および保全生物学者, 北アリゾナ大学の教授》

□ **concept** 名①概念, 観念, テーマ ②(計画案などの)基本的な方向

□ **concern** 動①関係する,《be -ed in [with] ~》~に関係している ②心配させる,《be -ed about [for] ~》~を心配する 名①関心事 ②関心, 心配 ③関係, 重要性

□ **conclude** 動①終える, 完結する ②結論を下す

□ **conclusion** 名結論, 結末

□ **concrete** 形具体的な, 明確な

□ **condition** 名①(健康)状態, 境遇 ②《-s》状況, 様子 ③条件

□ **conditional** 形条件付きの, 条件としての

□ **conduct** 動①指導する ②実施する, 処理[処置]する

□ **conference** 名①会議, 協議, 相談 ②協議会

□ **confirmation** 名確認, 確証

□ **confirmation bias** 確証バイアス《仮説や信念を検証する際にそれを支持する情報ばかりを集め, 反証する情報を無視または集めようとしない傾向のこと》

□ **confuse** 動混同する, 困惑させる, 混乱させる

□ **confusing** 形混乱させる, 紛らわしい

□ **connect** 動つながる, つなぐ, 関係づける

□ **connected** 動connect(つながる)の過去, 過去分詞 形結合した, 関係のある

□ **connection** 名①つながり, 関係 ②縁故

□ **connectionist** 名コネクショニスト《コネクショニズムモデルに基づいた研究アプローチを取る研究者》

□ **connectionist AI** コネクショニストAI《一般的には, ニューラルネットワーク型AIを指す》

□ **conquer** 動征服する, 制圧する

□ **conscious** 形①(状況などを)意識している, 自覚している ②意識のある

□ **consciousness** 名意識, 自覚, 気づいていること

□ **consecutive** 形 連続した

□ **consequence** 名 結果，成り行き

□ **conservation** 名 保護，保管，保存

□ **conservation biology** 保全生態学

□ **consider** 動 ①考慮する，～しようと思う ②（～と）みなす ③気にかける，思いやる

□ **consist** 動 ①《－of ～》（部分・要素から）成る ②《－in ～》～に存在する，～にある

□ **consistently** 副 首尾一貫して，連続して，あくまで，毅然として

□ **consonant** 名 子音，子音字

□ **consonant-heavy** 形 子音を多用した，子音中心の

□ **constraint** 名 制限，制約，抑制，強制

□ **construct** 動 建設する，組み立てる

□ **consumption** 名 ①消費，消費量 ②食べること

□ **contain** 動 ①含む，入っている ②（感情などを）抑える

□ **content** 名 ①《-s》中身，内容，目次 ②満足

□ **content-addressable memory** 連想メモリ《コンピューターなどの記憶装置（メモリ）の一種で，たいていの一般的なメモリは整数値などでアドレスを指定してその内容を読み書きするものであるのに対し，内容（の一部）を指定して，そのアドレスあるいは内容全体を読み出すことができる》

□ **contestant** 名 （競技会・コンテストへの）出場者

□ **context** 名 文脈，前後関係，コンテクスト

□ **continuous** 形 連続的な，継続する，絶え間ない

□ **continuously** 副 連続して，絶え間なく，変わりなく

□ **contribute** 動 ①貢献する ②寄稿する ③寄付する

□ **contributor** 名 寄付者，貢献者，寄稿者

□ **control** 動 ①管理［支配］する ②抑制する，コントロールする 名 ①管理，支配（力） ②抑制 **in control** ～を支配して，～を掌握している **out of control** コントロールできない，手に負えない **take control of** ～を制御［管理］する，支配する

□ **convenient** 形 便利な，好都合な

□ **convention** 名 ①慣習，しきたり ②会議，集会，大会 ③協定

□ **conventional** 形 習慣的な

□ **conversation** 名 会話，会談

□ **conversational** 形 会話の，対話型の

□ **converse** 動 （打ち解けて）話す，会話する

□ **convince** 動 納得させる，確信させる

□ **convolutional** 形 畳み込みの

□ **convolutional neural network (CNN)** 畳み込みニューラルネットワーク《層間を共通重みの局所結合で繋いだニューラルネットワークの総称・クラス。機械学習，特に画像や動画認識に広く使われる》

□ **cope** 動 うまく処理する，対処する

□ **copy** 名 ①コピー，写し ②（書籍の）一部，冊 ③広告文 動 写す，まねる，コピーする

□ **cord** 名 ひも，コード

□ **Corinna Cortes** コリーナ・コルテス《機械学習への貢献で知られるデンマークのコンピューター科学者，現在GoogleResearchの責任者》

□ **corner** 熟 **around the corner** すぐ近くに

□ **corporation** 名 法人，（株式）会社，公団，社団法人

□ **correct** 形正しい，適切な，りっぱな

□ **correctly** 副正しく，正確に

□ **corresponding** 形一致する，符合する，通信の

□ **cost** 名①値段，費用 ②損失，犠牲 **upfront cost** 初期費用 動（金・費用が）かかる，（～を）要する，（人に金額を）費やさせる

□ **cost-benefit** 形費用と便益の（関係の）

□ **could** 熟 **If**＋《主語》＋**could** ～できればなあ《仮定法》**could have done** ～だったかもしれない《仮定法》

□ **council** 名会議，評議会，議会

□ **count** 動①数える ②（～を…と）みなす ③重要［大切］である

□ **Covid-19** 名新型コロナウイルス感染症

□ **cow** 名雌牛，乳牛

□ **coworker** 名（職場の）同僚

□ **crash** 名激突，墜落

□ **create** 動創造する，生み出す，引き起こす

□ **creation** 名創造［物］

□ **creative** 形創造力のある，独創的な

□ **creativity** 名創造性，独創力

□ **creature** 名（神の）創造物，生物，動物

□ **credit** 名①信用，評判，名声 ②掛け売り，信用貸し

□ **creepy** 形むずむずする，ぞっとする，気味が悪い

□ **Crete** 名クレタ島《ギリシャ共和国南方の地中海に浮かぶ同国最大の島。古代ミノア文明が栄えた土地で，クノッソス宮殿をはじめとする多くの遺跡を持つ》

□ **crime** 名①（法律上の）罪，犯罪 ②悪事，よくない行為

□ **criminal** 形犯罪の，罪深い，恥ずべき 名犯罪者，犯人

□ **crisis** 名①危機，難局 ②重大局面

□ **criteria** 名基準《criterionの複数形》

□ **crop** 名作物，収穫

□ **culprit** 名犯人

□ **cupboard** 名食器棚，戸棚

□ **curiously** 副①不思議なことに ②もの珍しそうに

□ **current** 形現在の，目下の，通用［流通］している

□ **currently** 副今のところ，現在

□ **curvy** 形曲がりくねった

□ **customer** 名顧客

□ **cutting-edge** 形最先端の［を行く］

□ **cyberpunk** 名サイバーパンク

□ **cybersecurity** 名サイバー・セキュリティー

□ **Czech** 形チェコ（共和国）の

D

□ **daily** 形毎日の，日常の

□ **dairy** 名搾乳所，酪農場，乳製品販売［製造］所

□ **DALL-E** 名DALL-E《画像生成AIツール。自然言語の記述からデジタル画像を生成するためにOpenAIによって開発されたディープ ラーニングモデル》

□ **dare** 動《－to ～》思い切って［あえて］～する

□ **darker-skinned** 形より浅黒い肌の

□ **Dartmouth College** ダートマス大学

□ **Dartmouth Summer Research Project on Artificial Intelligence (DSRPAI)** ダートマス会議《人工知

能という学術研究分野を確立した会議の通称。人類史上初めて「人工知能(Artificial Intelligence)」という用語が使われたとされる。1956年》

□ **data** 名 データ, 情報 **big data** ビッグデータ《人間では全体を把握することが困難な巨大なデータ群のこと》 **raw data** 加工されていないデータ, 未加工データ, 生データ, 原資料 **sequential data** 順次データ

□ **dataset** 名 データセット《データの集合のこと》

□ **David Ferrucci** デイビット・フェルッチ《アメリカ合衆国のコンピューター科学者。テレビのクイズ番組Jeopardy! で優勝したWatson コンピューター システムの開発において, IBM と学術研究者およびエンジニアのチームの主任研究員を務めた》

□ **David Rumehlart** デビッド・ラメルハート《アメリカの認知心理学者でニューラルネットワークの研究者。ニューラルネットワークの研究, 特にバックプロパゲーションと, ジェームズ・マクレランドらとともに提唱したPDPモデルが知られる。1942–2011》

□ **deadly** 形 命にかかわる, 痛烈な, 破壊的な

□ **deal** 動 ①分配する ②《– with [in] ～》～を扱う 名 ①取引, 扱い ②(不特定の)量, 額 **a good [great] deal (of ～)** かなり[ずいぶん・大量](の～), 多額(の～)

□ **death** 名 ①死, 死ぬこと ②《the –》終えん, 消滅

□ **DEC** 略 ディジタル・イクイップメント・コーポレーション《かつてアメリカ合衆国を代表したコンピューター企業の一つ。Digital Equipment Corporationの略》

□ **decade** 名 10年間

□ **deception** 名 だますこと, 詐欺

□ **decide to do** ～することに決める

□ **decision** 名 ①決定, 決心 ②判決

□ **decision tree** 決定木《木構造を用いて分類や回帰を行う機械学習の手法の一つ》

□ **decision-making** 名 意思[政策・対策]決定

□ **decline** 動 ①断る ②傾く ③衰える

□ **deep AI** ディープAI《強いAI(Strong AI)の言い換え》

□ **Deep Blue** ディープ・ブルー《IBMが開発したチェス専用のスーパーコンピューター。ディープ・ソートを破った当時チェスの世界チャンピオンだった, ガルリ・カスパロフを打ち負かすことを目標として1989年より開発》

□ **Deep Fritz** ディープ・フリッツ《フランツ・モルシュとマシアス・ファイストとが設計したチェスソフト「フリッツ」のマルチプロセッサ版》

□ **Deep Junior** ディープ・ジュニア《イスラエルのプログラマーによるコンピューターチェス・プログラム「ジュニア」のマルチプロセッサ版》

□ **deep learning** ディープラーニング《十分なデータ量があれば, 人間の力なしに機械が自動的にデータから特徴を抽出してくれるディープニューラルネットワーク(DNN)を用いた学習のこと》

□ **deep neural network** ディープニューラルネットワーク《ニューラルネットワークをディープラーニングに対応させて4層以上に層を深くしたもの》

□ **deep structured learning** 深層学習《人間の脳神経回路の仕組みをモデルにした機械学習手法》

□ **Deep Thought** ディープ・ソート《アメリカ合衆国で開発されたチェスコンピューター。 カーネギー・メロン大学で許峰雄らにより開発され, IBMで開発が継続された》

□ **deepfake** 名 ディープフェイク《deep learning (深層学習)の技術を応用して, 本物にそっくりなfake (偽

物）の映像や音声を作りだすこと》

□ **deeply** 副深く，非常に

□ **DeepMind (Technologies)** ディープマインド・テクノロジーズ《イギリスにあるAlphabetの人工知能子会社。2010年にDeepMind Technologiesとして起業され，2014年にGoogleによって買収された》

□ **defeat** 動 ①打ち破る，負かす ②だめにする

□ **defenseless** 形無防備の，防御手段がない

□ **deficiency** 名 ①欠乏，不足 ②欠損症

□ **define** 動 ①定義する，限定する ②〜の顕著な特性である

□ **definition** 名定義，限定

□ **degree** 名 ①程度，階級，位，身分 ②（温度・角度の）度

□ **delay** 動遅らせる，延期する

□ **deliver** 動 ①配達する，伝える ②達成する，果たす

□ **delusional** 形妄想の［に関する］，妄想的な

□ **democracy** 名民主主義，民主政治

□ **demographics** 名人口統計学，人口動態，人口構成

□ **demonstrate** 動 ①デモをする ②実演する ③実証する

□ **demonstration** 名 ①論証，証明 ②デモンストレーション，実演 ③デモ，示威運動

□ **depend** 動《– on [upon] 〜》①〜を頼る，〜をあてにする ②〜による

□ **dependent** 形頼っている，〜次第である

□ **deploy** 動配備［配置・展開］する

□ **depressed** 形がっかりした，落胆した

□ **depth** 名深さ，奥行き，深いところ

□ **describe** 動（言葉で）描写する，特色を述べる，説明する

□ **description** 名（言葉で）記述（すること），描写（すること）

□ **deserve** 動（〜を）受けるに足る，値する，（〜して）当然である

□ **design** 動設計する，企てる 名デザイン，設計（図）

□ **desire** 名欲望，欲求，願望

□ **desktop** 形デスクトップの

□ **despite** 前〜にもかかわらず

□ **destroy** 動破壊する，絶滅させる，無効にする

□ **destruction** 名破壊（行為・状態）

□ **detailed** 形詳細な，詳しい

□ **detect** 動見つける

□ **detection** 名発見，探知，検出

□ **determine** 動 ①決心する［させる］ ②決定する［させる］ ③測定する

□ **develop** 動 ①発達する［させる］ ②開発する

□ **developer** 名開発者，宅地開発業者，デベロッパー

□ **development** 名 ①発達，発展 ②開発 **research and development** 研究開発

□ **deviation** 名 ①（進路・本筋などから）それること ②逸脱，脱線 ③偏差値

□ **device** 名 ①工夫 ②案 ③装置

□ **dialect** 名方言，なまり

□ **dialogue** 名対話，話し合い

□ **dictionary** 名辞書，辞典

□ **Dietrich Prinz** ディートリッヒ・プリンツ《コンピューターサイエンスのパイオニアであり，特に1951年に最初の限定チェスプログラムを開発した》

□ **difficulty** 名 ①むずかしさ ②難局，支障，苦情，異議 ③《-ties》財政困難

□ **diffusion** 名拡散，発散

□ **digital** 形 ①数字の，数字表示の，

デジタルの ②指の, 指状の

☐ **digital assistant** デジタル・アシスタント《通常はインターネットを介して, 利用者との会話をシミュレートする高度なコンピューター・プログラム》

☐ **Digital Equipment Corporation (DEC)** ディジタル・イクイップメント・コーポレーション《かつてアメリカ合衆国を代表したコンピューター企業の一つ》

☐ **digitally** 副デジタル処理で

☐ **digitized** 形デジタル化する

☐ **dimension** 名寸法, 大きさ, 次元

☐ **dimensionality** 名次元(性)

☐ **dimensionality reduction** 次元削減《高次元空間から低次元空間へデータを変換しながら, 低次元表現が元データの何らかの意味ある特性を保持すること》

☐ **direct** 形まっすぐな, 直接の, 率直な, 露骨な

☐ **direction** 名①方向, 方角 ②《-s》指示, 説明書 ③指導, 指揮

☐ **directly** 副①じかに ②まっすぐに ③ちょうど

☐ **director** 名管理者, 指導者, 監督

☐ **disadvantage** 名不利な立場[条件], 損失

☐ **disappointed** 形がっかりした, 失望した

☐ **discovery** 名発見

☐ **discrepancy** 名差異, 相違, 矛盾

☐ **discrete** 形(完全に)別々の, 個別の

☐ **discrete value** 離散値

☐ **discriminate** 動①見分ける, 識別する, 区別する ②差別する

☐ **discriminatory** 形差別的な

☐ **discuss** 動議論[検討]する

☐ **discussion** 名討議, 討論

☐ **disease** 名①病気 ②(社会や精神の)不健全な状態

☐ **disinformation** 名偽情報, 虚報, がせネタ, デマ

☐ **display** 名展示, 陳列, 表出

☐ **dissident** 名意見の異なる人, 批判者, 反体制の人

☐ **distance** 名距離, 隔たり, 遠方

☐ **distinct** 形①独特な ②はっきりした

☐ **distinguish** 動①見分ける, 区別する ②特色づける ③相違を見分ける

☐ **dive** 動①飛び込む, もぐる ②急降下する[させる]

☐ **divide** 動分かれる, 分ける, 割れる, 割る

☐ **DNA sequencing** DNA塩基配列決定法

☐ **doctoral** 形博士(号)の, 権威のある

☐ **doctorate** 名博士号

☐ **dolphin** 名イルカ

☐ **domain** 名①統治地域, 領土 ②領域, 分野 ③(インターネットの)ドメイン **public domain** パブリックドメイン《著作物や発明などの知的創作物について, 知的財産権が発生していない状態または消滅した状態のこと》

☐ **dominant** 形支配的な, 優勢な, (遺伝において)優性な

☐ **dominate** 動支配する, 統治する, 優位を占める

☐ **Donald Hebb** ドナルド・ヘッブ《カナダの心理学者。神経心理学の開拓者の一人であり, ニューラルネットワーク研究の先駆者でもある。ヘッブの法則でその名を知られる。1904–1985》

☐ **Donald Michie** ドナルド・ミッキー《イギリスの人工知能研究者。1923–2007》

☐ **dot** 名①点, 小数点 ②水玉(模様)

☐ **dozen** 名1ダース, 12(個)

☐ **draft** 名 ①下書き，草稿 ②図案，下絵

☐ **draw** 動 ①引く，引っ張る ②描く ③引き分けになる［する］

☐ **dream of** ～を夢見る

☐ **drew** 動 draw（引く）の過去

☐ **dried** 動 dry（乾燥する）の過去，過去分詞

☐ **driver** 名 ①運転手 ②（馬車の）御者

☐ **driving** 名 運転

☐ **drone** 名 ドローン

☐ **drove** 動 drive（車で行く）の過去

☐ **drug** 名 薬，麻薬，麻酔薬

☐ **DSRPAI** 略 ダートマス会議《人工知能という学術研究分野を確立した会議の通称。人類史上初めて「人工知能（Artificial Intelligence）」という用語が使われたとされる。1956年。Dartmouth Summer Research Project on Artificial Intelligenceの略》

☐ **due** 形 予定された，期日のきている，支払われるべき **due to** ～によって，～が原因で

☐ **dull** 形 退屈な，鈍い，くすんだ，ぼんやりした

☐ **duplex** 名 二世帯用住宅，デュプレックス《双方向に送信可能な通信方式》，二本鎖

☐ **dystopia** 名 ディストピア，暗黒郷

E

☐ **E.D.M.** 略 エレクトロニック・ダンス・ミュージック

☐ **e.g.** 略 例えば

☐ **each one** 各自

☐ **each other** お互いに

☐ **eager** 形 ①熱心な ②《be – for ～》～を切望している，《be – to ～》しきりに～したがっている

☐ **eager (learner)** 熱心な学習《教師データから何かしらの新しい方程式を作り出すタイプの学習アルゴリズム》

☐ **earn** 動 ①儲ける，稼ぐ ②（名声を）博す

☐ **ease** 名 安心，気楽

☐ **easily** 副 ①容易に，たやすく，苦もなく ②気楽に

☐ **echo** 名 こだま，反響

☐ **e-commerce** 名 電子商取引，eコマース

☐ **e-commerce site** 電子商取引サイト，ECサイト

☐ **economist** 名 ①経済学者 ②倹約家

☐ **economy** 名 ①経済，財政 ②節約

☐ **Ed Asner** エドワード・アズナー《アメリカ合衆国の俳優・声優。1929–2021》

☐ **edge** 名 ①刃 ②端，縁

☐ **edge case** エッジケース《極端な動作パラメータでのみ発生する問題または状況》

☐ **educable** 形 学習能力のある，訓練可能な

☐ **effect** 名 ①影響，効果，結果 ②実施，発効 **ELIZA effect** イライザ効果《自然な会話を行う機械を目の前にした時，本物の人間と対話しているかのような錯覚に陥ってしまう現象》 **in effect** 有効な，事実上 **side effect** 副作用，副次的影響

☐ **efficacy** 名（薬などの）効きめ，効能

☐ **effort** 名 努力（の成果）

☐ **El Ajedrecista** エル・アヘドレシスタ《レオナルド・トーレス・ケベードが1912年に発明したチェスのオートマタ》

☐ **election** 名 選挙，投票

☐ **electric** 形 電気の，電動の

☐ **electronic** 形 電子工学の，エレク

トロニクスの

☐ **element** 名要素, 成分, 元素

☐ **elephantine** 形 ①象の ②巨大な, 強大な

☐ **elephantitis** 名象皮病

☐ **ELIZA** 名イライザ《ジョセフ・ワイゼンバウムによって開発された, いわゆる人工無脳の起源となった対話型自然言語処理プログラム》

☐ **ELIZA effect** イライザ効果《自然な会話を行う機械を目の前にした時, 本物の人間と対話しているかのような錯覚に陥ってしまう現象》

☐ **Ellen** 名エレン《人名》

☐ **email** 名Eメール

☐ **embryo** 名 ①(発達の)初期, 初期段階 ②胚, 胎児

☐ **emergency** 形緊急の

☐ **employee** 名従業員, 会社員, 被雇用者

☐ **empress** 名女帝, 皇后, 女王

☐ **enable** 動(～することを)可能にする, 容易にする

☐ **enact** 動実行[実施]する

☐ **encourage** 動 ①勇気づける ②促進する, 助長する

☐ **end** 熟 **at the end of** ～の終わりに **in the end** とうとう, 結局, ついに

☐ **enemy** 名敵

☐ **enforcement** 名(法律などの)施行

☐ **engage** 動(活動に)従事する **engaged with** ～と関わりあう

☐ **engine** 名エンジン, 機関, (精巧な)機械装置

☐ **engineer** 名技師

☐ **engineering** 名工学

☐ **English-language** 形英語の

☐ **enhanced** 形改良[改善・強化]された

☐ **ENIAC** 略ENIAC(エニアック)《アメリカで開発された黎明期の電子計算機》

☐ **enough** 動 **have had enough** こりごり, もうたくさん

☐ **ensure** 動確実にする, 保証する

☐ **entertainment** 名 ①楽しみ, 娯楽 ②もてなし, 歓待

☐ **entire** 形全体の, 完全な, まったくの

☐ **entirely** 副完全に, まったく

☐ **entitled** 形称号を与えられた

☐ **entity** 名実在する物, 実体

☐ **environment** 名 ①環境 ②周囲(の状況), 情勢

☐ **episode** 名 ①挿話, 出来事 ②(テレビ番組の)1回放映分 ③(シリーズ物の)第～話

☐ **EquBot** 名エクボット社《AI Powered Equity ETFの運用モデルを開発。実質的な運用も担っている》

☐ **equipment** 名装置, 機材, 道具, 設備

☐ **equity** 名 ①公正 ②株主資本 ③株(式)

☐ **era** 名時代, 年代

☐ **error** 名誤り, 間違い, 過失

☐ **essential** 形本質的な, 必須の

☐ **essentially** 副本質的に, 原則的に, 本来

☐ **establish** 動確立する, 立証する, 設置[設立]する

☐ **estate** 名不動産, 財産, 遺産, 地所, 土地 **real estate** 不動産, 土地

☐ **ETF** 略上場投資信託《金融商品取引所で取引される投資信託。exchange traded fundの略》

☐ **ethical** 形倫理の, 道徳的な

☐ **EU** 略EU[欧州連合]

☐ **Eugene Onegin** 『エヴゲーニイ・オネーギン』《アレクサンドル・プーシキンの韻文小説》

☐ **Eugenia Kuyda** ユーゲニア・ク

イダ《Luka Co-founder & CEO。ロシア出身。AIと何気ない会話ができるスマートフォンのアプリ「レプリカ」を開発》

□ **evaluate** 動 ①価値をはかる ②評価する，査定する

□ **evaluator** 名 評価する人

□ **Evelyn Fix** イブリン・フィックス《アメリカ合衆国の統計家》

□ **even though** ～であるけれども，～にもかかわらず

□ **eventual** 形 起こりうる，結局の

□ **eventually** 副 結局は

□ **every other** 1つおきの～，他のすべての

□ **every time** ～するときはいつも

□ **everyday** 形 毎日の，日々の

□ **everything** 代 すべてのこと［もの］，何でも，何もかも

□ **everywhere** 副 どこにいても，いたるところに

□ **evidence** 名 ①証拠，証人 ②形跡

□ **evolve** 動 進化する［させる］，発展する［させる］

□ **examine** 動 試験する，調査［検査］する，診察する

□ **example** 熟 **for example** たとえば

□ **except** 前 ～を除いて，～のほかは 接 ～ということを除いて

□ **exception** 名 例外，除外，異論

□ **exceptional** 形 例外的な，特別に優れた

□ **exchange traded fund (ETF)** 上場投資信託《金融商品取引所で取引される投資信託》

□ **excited** 形 興奮した，わくわくした

□ **excitement** 名 興奮（すること）

□ **exclusion** 名 排除，除外

□ **exclusion bias** 除外バイアス《調査対象から特定の年齢層や人種・民族を除外する，あるいはデータが入手しやすいとの理由のみで調査対象を選出することによって生じる偏り》

□ **execute** 動 ①実行する，執行する ②死刑にする

□ **executive** 名 ①高官，実行委員 ②重役，役員，幹部

□ **exercise** 名 ①運動，体操 ②練習 動 ①運動する，練習する ②影響を及ぼす

□ **exist** 動 存在する，生存する，ある，いる

□ **existence** 名 存在，実在，生存

□ **existing** 形 現存の，現在の，現行の

□ **expand** 動 ①広げる，拡張［拡大］する ②発展させる，拡充する

□ **expect** 動 予期［予測］する，（当然のこととして）期待する

□ **experiment** 名 実験，試み

□ **expert** 名 専門家，熟練者，エキスパート **oncology expert**《病理》がん［腫瘍］専門医 形 熟練した，専門の

□ **expert system** エキスパートシステム《人工知能研究から生まれたコンピューターシステムで，人間の専門家の意思決定能力をエミュレートするもの》

□ **exploit** 動 ①開発する，活用する ②搾取する，不当に利用する

□ **explore** 動 探検［調査］する，切り開く

□ **explosion** 名 爆発，急増 **intelligence explosion** 知性爆発《「技術的特異点（シンギュラリティ）」に代わる新語》

□ **exposed** 形 露出した

□ **exposure** 名 ①さらされる ②暴露，暴くこと

□ **express** 動 表現する，述べる

□ **expression** 名 ①表現，表示，表情 ②言い回し，語句 **gene expression** 遺伝子発現《遺伝子がもっている遺伝情報が，さまざまな生体機能をもつた

んぱく質の合成を通じて具体的に現れること》

□ **expressive** 形表している, 表情豊かな

□ **extreme** 形極端な, 極度の, いちばん端の

□ **extremely** 副非常に, 極度に

F

□ **fabric** 名①織物, 生地 ②構造

□ **Facebook** 名フェイスブック

□ **facial** 形顔の, 顔に用いる

□ **facial recognition** 顔認識

□ **facial-recognition** 形顔認識の

□ **fact** 熟 **in fact** つまり, 実は, 要するに

□ **factory** 名工場, 製造所

□ **fail** 動①失敗する, 落第する［させる］②《－to ～》～し損なう, ～できない ③失望させる

□ **failure** 名①失敗, 落第 ②不足, 欠乏 ③停止, 減退

□ **fair** 形①正しい, 公平［正当］な ②快晴の ③色白の, 金髪の ④かなりの ⑤《古》美しい 名〔農産物や商品の〕見本市, 品評会

□ **fairly** 副①公平に ②かなり, 相当に

□ **fake** 形にせの

□ **fall back** 後退する, 戻る

□ **false** 形うその, 間違った, にせの, 不誠実な

□ **familiar** 形①親しい, 親密な ②《be－with ～》～に精通している ③普通の, いつもの, おなじみの

□ **far** 熟 **how far** どのくらいの距離か **so far** 今までのところ, これまでは

□ **farm** 熟 **vertical farm** 垂直農園

□ **farmer** 名農民, 農場経営者

□ **farming** 名農業, 農作業 **vertical farming** 垂直農法《高層建築物の階層, 及び高層の傾斜面を使用して垂直的に農作業, 動物の育成を行う方法》

□ **farm-raised** 形（動物が）農場で飼育された

□ **fascism** 名ファシズム

□ **fatal** 形致命的な, 運命を決する

□ **fate** 名①運命, 宿命 ②破滅, 悲運

□ **faulty** 形欠陥のある, 不完全な

□ **fear** 名①恐れ ②心配, 不安 動①恐れる ②心配する

□ **feature** 名①特徴, 特色 ②顔の一部, 《-s》顔立ち ③（ラジオ・テレビ・新聞などの）特集

□ **feature-length movie** 〈主に米〉長編映画

□ **feed** 名①飼育, 食事 ②供給

□ **feedback** 名反響, フィードバック

□ **feed-forward** 名フィードフォワード, 正方向送り

□ **feed-forward neural network (FNN)** 順伝播型ニューラルネットワーク《データがネットワークを構成する層の間を一方向（入力層から出力層へ）にしか流れない。前の層から次の層へと, 順番に伝播していくネットワーク》

□ **feeling** 名①感じ, 気持ち ②触感, 知覚 ③同情, 思いやり, 感受性

□ **female** 形女性の, 婦人の, 雌の 名婦人, 雌

□ **feminist** 名フェミニスト

□ **Feng-Hsiung Hsu** 許 峰雄《きょ ほうゆう, 台湾出身のアメリカ合衆国の計算機科学者。チェスコンピューターの「ディープ・ソート」や「ディープ・ブルー」の主要設計者の一人》

□ **Ferranti Mark 1** フェランティマーク1《世界初の商用汎用電子式コンピューター》

□ **fiction** 名フィクション, 作り話, 小説

□ **Fifth Symphony** （ベートーヴ

ェンの）第5交響曲

☐ **figure** 動 ①描写する，想像する ②計算する ③目立つ，（～として）現れる **figure out** 理解する，～であるとわかる，（原因などを）解明する

☐ **filled with** 《be –》～でいっぱいになる

☐ **film** 名 フィルム，映画

☐ **final** 形 最後の，決定的な

☐ **finance** 名 ①財政，財務 ②（銀行からの）資金，融資 ③《-s》財政状態，財源

☐ **financial** 形 ①財務（上）の，金融（上）の ②金融関係者の

☐ **financial-related** 形 金融関連の

☐ **find out** 見つけ出す，気がつく，知る，調べる，解明する

☐ **Finnish** 形 フィンランド（人［語］）の

☐ **firm** 形 堅い，しっかりした，断固とした

☐ **firmly** 副 しっかりと，断固として

☐ **first** 熟 **at first** 最初は，初めのうちは **for the first time** 初めて

☐ **fit** 形 ①適当な，相応な ②体の調子がよい

☐ **five stars** 五つ星

☐ **fix** 動 ①固定する［させる］ ②修理する ③決定する ④用意する，整える

☐ **fixed** 形 ①固定した，ゆるぎない ②八百長の

☐ **flood** 動 ①氾濫する，氾濫させる ②殺到する

☐ **flour** 名 小麦粉，粉末

☐ **flowchart** 名 フローチャート，流れ図

☐ **FNN** 略 順伝播型ニューラルネットワーク《データがネットワークを構成する層の間を一方向（入力層から出力層へ）にしか流れない。前の層から次の層へと，順番に伝播していくネットワーク。feed-forward neural networkの略》

☐ **focus** 名 ①焦点，ピント ②関心の的，着眼点 ③中心 動 ①焦点を合わせる ②（関心・注意を）集中させる

☐ **fold** 動 ①折りたたむ，包む ②（手を）組む

☐ **folder** 名 フォルダー《ファイルなどの格納場所》

☐ **folklore** 名 民間伝承

☐ **following** 形 《the –》次の，次に続く

☐ **for** 熟 **for a while** しばらくの間，少しの間 **for all ～** ～にもかかわらず **for example** たとえば **for oneself** 独力で，自分のために **for the first time** 初めて **for ～ years** ～年間，～年にわたって

☐ **force** 名 力，勢い

☐ **forecast** 名 予想，予測，天気予報，先見

☐ **forest** 熟 **random (decision) forest** ランダムフォレスト《複数の決定木を組み合わせ，汎化能力を高めた頑健で実用的なアルゴリズム》

☐ **forex** 名 外国為替，外為《= foreign exchange》

☐ **form** 名 ①形，形式 ②書式 動 形づくる

☐ **former** 形 ①前の，先の，以前の ②《the –》（二者のうち）前者の

☐ **formerly** 副 元は，以前は

☐ **fortunately** 副 幸運にも

☐ **forward** 形 ①前方の，前方へ向かう ②将来の ③先の 副 ①前方に ②将来に向けて ③先へ，進んで

☐ **foundation** 名 ①建設，創設 ②基礎，土台

☐ **founder** 名 創立者，設立者

☐ **4chan** 名 4chan《2ちゃんねる創設者の西村博之が管理・運営する，主に英語圏を対象とした世界最大規模の画像掲示板。2003年10月1日開設》

☐ **fraction** 名 ごく少量，一部分，端数

☐ **franchise** 名（映画・テレビドラマ

などの）シリーズ

☐ **Frank Rosenblatt** フランク・ローゼンブラット《アメリカ合衆国の心理学者でニューラルネット研究の開拓者のひとり。パーセプトロンを開発。1928–1971》

☐ **Frankenstein** 名『フランケンシュタイン』《ゴシック小説。原題は『フランケンシュタイン，あるいは現代のプロメテウス』（Frankenstein: or The Modern Prometheus），1818年》

☐ **Frankenstein's monster** フランケンシュタイン博士が創造した怪物

☐ **fraud** 名詐欺［ペテン］行為

☐ **fraudulent** 形（行為や金などが）詐欺的な，不正な

☐ **freedom** 名 ①自由 ②束縛がないこと

☐ **freely** 副自由に，障害なしに

☐ **French** 形フランス（人・語）の 名①フランス語 ②《the –》フランス人

☐ **frequency** 名 ①頻繁に起こること，頻発 ②頻度 ③周波数

☐ **frequent** 形ひんぱんな，よくある

☐ **frequently** 副頻繁に，しばしば

☐ **friendly** 形親しみのある，親切な，友情のこもった

☐ **frustrated** 形挫折した，失望した

☐ **fulfill** 動（義務・約束を）果たす，（要求・条件を）満たす

☐ **full of** 《be –》～で一杯である

☐ **fully** 副十分に，完全に，まるまる

☐ **function** 名機能，作用 **activation function** 活性化関数《ニューラルネットワークのニューロンにおける，入力のなんらかの合計（しばしば，線形な重み付け総和）から，出力を決定するための関数で，非線形な関数とすることが多い》

☐ **functionality** 名（プログラムなどの）機能

☐ **fund** 名 ①資金，基金，財源 ②金 ③公債，国債

☐ **fundamental** 形基本の，根本的な，重要な

☐ **funding** 名 ①財源 ②財政支援 ③資金調達

☐ **fungal** 形（菌類のように）急に発生する

☐ **funny** 形 ①おもしろい，こっけいな ②奇妙な，うさんくさい

☐ **further** 形いっそう遠い，その上の，なおいっそうの 副いっそう遠く，その上に，もっと

☐ **furthermore** 副さらに，その上

☐ **future** 熟 **in the future** 将来は

G

☐ **gain** 動 ①得る，増す ②進歩する，進む

☐ **game** 熟 **zero-sum game** ゼロサムゲーム《参加者全員の負け分，勝ち分の総和がゼロになるゲーム。チェスや囲碁など》

☐ **Game of Life, The** 人生ゲーム《1960年にアメリカ Milton Bradley 社（現・ハズブロ）から発売されたボードゲーム。日本でも1968年にタカラトミーから発売》

☐ **game-changing** 形現状を打破する，革新的な

☐ **gaming** 名コンピューターゲームをプレイすること

☐ **Garry Kasparov** ガルリ・カスパロフ《アゼルバイジャンのバクー出身の元チェス選手。15年もの間チェスの世界チャンピオンのタイトルを保持し続けた。1963–》

☐ **gather** 動 ①集まる，集める ②生じる，増す ③推測する

☐ **gender** 名（社会的に決められた）性，性別

☐ **gender classification**

algorithms 自動性別分類アルゴリズム

□ **gene** 名 遺伝子

□ **gene expression** 遺伝子発現《遺伝子がもっている遺伝情報が，さまざまな生体機能をもつたんぱく質の合成を通じて具体的に現れること》

□ **general** 形 ①全体の，一般の，普通の ②おおよその ③(職位の)高い，上級の 名 **in general** 一般に，たいてい

□ **generalize** 動 一般化する，概括する，一般論を述べる

□ **generally** 副 ①一般に，だいたい ②たいてい

□ **general-purpose** 形 汎用(の)

□ **generate** 動 生み出す，引き起こす

□ **generative** 形《言語学》生成的な，文を生成する

□ **Generative Pre-trained Transformer 3 (GPT-3)** GPT-3《OpenAIが開発した，1750億個のパラメータを使用した『文章生成言語モデル』》

□ **generator** 名 発電機，発生器

□ **genius** 名 天才，才能

□ **genre** 名 ①ジャンル，分野，形式，類型 ②風俗画

□ **geofence** 名 地理上のフェンス《地図上でエリアを限定する仮想的な壁》

□ **German** 形 ドイツ(人・語)の 名 ①ドイツ人 ②ドイツ語

□ **get back** 戻る，帰る

□ **get to** (事)を始める，～に達する[到着する]

□ **get used to** ～になじむ，～に慣れる

□ **giant** 名 巨人，大男

□ **gift** 名 ①贈り物 ②(天賦の)才能

□ **give up on** ～に見切りをつける

□ **global** 形 地球(上)の，地球規模の，世界的な，国際的な

□ **glorification** 名 賛美

□ **glucose** 名 ブドウ糖，グルコース

□ **go** 熟 **go about one's daily business** 日々を送る，日常生活を続ける **go around** 広まる，まん延する **go back to** ～に帰る[戻る]，～に遡る，(中断していた作業に)再び取り掛かる **go for** ～に出かける，～を追い求める，～を好む **go on** 続く，続ける，進み続ける，起こる，発生する **go up against** (対戦相手・上司など)に立ち向かう **go wrong** 失敗する，道を踏みはずす，調子が悪くなる **same goes for**《the –》～についても同じことが言える

□ **goalpost** 名 (フットボールなどの)ゴールポスト，ゴールの支柱 **move the goalposts** (特に秘密裏に)規則や条件を変える，後から決定を覆す

□ **golem** 名 ゴーレム《ユダヤ教の伝承に登場する自分で動く泥人形》

□ **good at**《be –》～が得意だ

□ **Google** 名 グーグル

□ **Google Duplex** Google Duplex《Googleが2018年に発表した，AIを活用した自動音声通話技術による自動予約サービスで，リアルなAIとの会話を実現》

□ **gotten** 動 get(得る)の過去分詞

□ **Gottfried Wilhelm Leibniz** ゴットフリート・ヴィルヘルム・ライプニッツ《ドイツの哲学者，数学者。1646–1716》

□ **government** 名 政治，政府，支配

□ **GPT-2** 略 GPT-2《2019年2月にOpenAIによって作成されたTransformerをベースとしたテキスト生成モデル。GTP-3の前身》

□ **GPT-3** 略 GPT-3《OpenAIが開発した，1750億個のパラメータを使用した『文章生成言語モデル』。Generative Pretrained Transformerの略》

□ **graduate** 名 卒業生，(～学校の)出身者

☐ **grammar** 名文法

☐ **grammatical** 形文法上の，文法にのっとった

☐ **grand** 形雄大な，壮麗な

☐ **grandmaster** 名グランドマスター《国際チェス連盟（FIDE）により付与されるチェスのタイトル（称号）で，「世界チャンピオン」を別にすれば，チェス選手の最高位のタイトル》

☐ **graph** 名グラフ，図表

☐ **graphical** 形グラフィカル

☐ **graphical user interface (GUI)** グラフィカルユーザーインタフェース《コンピューターグラフィックスとポインティングデバイスなどを用いる，グラフィカル（ビジュアル）であることを特徴とするユーザーインタフェース》

☐ **Greek Mythology** ギリシャ神話

☐ **greenhouse** 名温室

☐ **greet** 動①あいさつする ②（喜んで）迎える

☐ **greeting** 名あいさつ（の言葉），あいさつ（状）

☐ **gripping** 形しっかりつかむ

☐ **Grogu** 名グローグー《『マンダロリアン』のキャラクター》

☐ **groundbreaking** 形革新的な，画期的な

☐ **grow into** 成長して～になる

☐ **growth** 名成長，発展

☐ **grunt** 名ぶうぶう言う声

☐ **GUI** 略グラフィカルユーザーインタフェース《コンピューターグラフィックスとポインティングデバイスなどを用いる，グラフィカル（ビジュアル）であることを特徴とするユーザーインタフェース。graphical user interfaceの略》

☐ **gunpowder** 名火薬

H

☐ **halfway** 形中間［中途］の，不完全な

☐ **hand** 熟 **on the other hand** 一方，他方では

☐ **handful** 名一握り，少量

☐ **handle** 動①手を触れる ②操縦する，取り扱う

☐ **hand-written** 形手書きの

☐ **happen to** たまたま～する，偶然～する

☐ **happy to do** 《be －》～してうれしい，喜んで～する

☐ **hard to** ～し難い

☐ **hardware** 名（コンピューターの）ハードウェア

☐ **harm** 名害，損害，危害

☐ **harmful** 形害を及ぼす，有害な

☐ **hate** 動嫌う，憎む，（～するのを）いやがる

☐ **hateful** 形憎らしい，忌まわしい

☐ **have** 熟 **could have done** ～だったかもしれない《仮定法》 **have no bearing on** ～に何の関係もない **should have done** ～すべきだった（のにしなかった）《仮定法》 **will have done** ～してしまっているだろう《未来完了形》

☐ **hawk** 名タカ（鷹）

☐ **hazard** 名危険，障害，ハザード

☐ **headline** 名（新聞などの）見出し

☐ **health care** 健康保険制度

☐ **healthcare** 名医療，健康管理

☐ **healthy** 形健康な，健全な，健康によい

☐ **hear of** ～について聞く

☐ **heat** 名①熱，暑さ ②熱気，熱意，激情

☐ **height** 名①高さ，身長 ②《the －》絶頂，真っ盛り ③高台，丘

☐ **hell** 名地獄，地獄のようなところ［状

態]

☐ **help out with** ～を手伝う

☐ **helpful** 形役に立つ，参考になる

☐ **Hephaestus** 名ヘーパイストス《ギリシア神話に登場する神。オリュンポス十二神の一柱》

☐ **Herbert A. Simon** ハーバート・アレクサンダー・サイモン《アメリカ合衆国の政治学者・認知心理学者・経営学者・情報科学者。心理学，人工知能，経営学，組織論，言語学，社会学，政治学，経済学，システム科学などに影響を与えた。1916–2001》

☐ **here and there** あちこちで

☐ **HFT** 略高頻度取引《1秒に満たないミリ秒単位のような極めて短い時間の間に，コンピューターでの自動的な株価のやり取り戦略を実施するシステムのこと。high-frequency trading の略》

☐ **hidden** 形隠れた，秘密の

☐ **hidden layer** 隠れ層

☐ **hierarchical** 形階級組織の，階層制の

☐ **high-dimensional** 形高次元の

☐ **high-frequency** 形高頻度の

☐ **high-frequency trading (HFT)** 高頻度取引《1秒に満たないミリ秒単位のような極めて短い時間の間に，コンピューターでの自動的な株価のやり取り戦略を実施するシステムのこと》

☐ **highlighted** 形脚光を浴びた，浮き彫りにされた

☐ **high-skilled** 形高度な技術を必要とする

☐ **high-tech** 形ハイテクの，先端技術の

☐ **highway** 名幹線道路，ハイウェー，本道

☐ **hire** 動雇う，賃借りする

☐ **historical** 形歴史の，歴史上の，史実に基づく

☐ **historical bias** 歴史的なバイアス《使用したデータが，もはや現在の現実を正確に反映していない場合に発生する》

☐ **historical** 形歴史の[に関する]

☐ **Hitler** 名ヒトラー

☐ **hoax** 名(人をだますための)でっち上げ，作り話

☐ **hobby** 名趣味，得意なこと

☐ **Hollywood-quality** 形ハリウッド並みの(品質の)

☐ **homelessness** 名(住む)家のないこと

☐ **Honda Legend** ホンダ・レジェンド《本田技研工業の高級セダン》

☐ **Hopfield network** ホップフィールド・ネットワーク《ニューラルネットワークの一モデル》

☐ **horror** 名①恐怖，ぞっとすること ②嫌悪

☐ **host** 名①客をもてなす主人 ②(テレビなどの)司会者

☐ **household** 名家族，世帯

☐ **how far** どのくらいの距離か

☐ **How to Speak Whale** 『How To Speak Whale: A Voyage into the Future of Animal Communication』《トム・マスティル著，2022年》

☐ **however** 副たとえ～でも 接けれども，だが

☐ **huge** 形巨大な，ばく大な

☐ **human-level** 名人間並みの

☐ **human-like** 形人間のような

☐ **humidity** 名湿度，湿気

☐ **hundreds of** 何百もの～

☐ **Hungarian** 形ハンガリー(人[語])の

☐ **Hydra** 名ヒドラ《アラブ首長国連邦のアブダビで世界最強を目指して作られていたチェス・マシーン》

☐ **hyperrealistic** 形超現実的な

I

□ **IBM** 名IBM社

□ **IBM 704 mainframe** IBM 704《IBMが1954年4月に発表した, 浮動小数点数演算ハードウェアを搭載した初の量産型コンピューター》

□ **IBM Research** IBM基礎研究所

□ **ID** 略身分証明(書)

□ **identify** 動①(本人・同一と)確認する, 見分ける ②意気投合する

□ **if** 熟 **If＋《主語》＋could** ～できればなあ《仮定法》 **as if** あたかも～のように, まるで～みたいに **what if** もし～だったらどうなるだろうか **wonder if** ～ではないかと思う

□ **illustration** 名①さし絵, イラスト ②図解 ③説明

□ **image** 名①印象, 姿 ②画像, 映像

□ **imageboard** 名画像掲示板

□ **imagine** 動想像する, 心に思い描く

□ **imitate** 動まねる, 模造する

□ **imitation** 名①模倣, まね ②模造品

□ **immediately** 副すぐに, ～するやいなや

□ **immortal** 形①死ぬことのない, 不死の ②不滅の

□ **impact** 名影響力, 反響, 効果

□ **imperfect** 形不完全な, 未完成な

□ **imperial** 形①帝国の, 皇帝の, 皇后の ②荘厳なる

□ **importance** 名重要性, 大切さ

□ **importantly** 副重大に, もったいぶって

□ **impress** 動印象づける, 感銘させる

□ **impressive** 形印象的な, 深い感銘を与える

□ **improve** 動改善する[させる], 進歩する

□ **improvement** 名改良, 改善

□ **in** 熟 **in a way** ある意味では **in addition** 加えて, さらに **in common** 共通して **in control** ～を支配して, ～を掌握している **in effect** 有効な, 事実上 **in fact** つまり, 実は, 要するに **in general** 一般に, たいてい **in order to** ～するために, ～しようと **in other words** すなわち, 言い換えれば **in terms of** ～の言葉で言えば, ～の点から **in the case of** ～の場合は **in the end** とうとう, 結局, ついに **in the future** 将来は **in the middle of** ～の真ん中[中ほど]に **in time** 間に合って, やがて

□ **inability** 名できないこと, 不能, 無力

□ **inappropriate** 形不適当な, まずい

□ **inbox** 名(電子メールの)受信トレイ

□ **incapable** 形(～が)できない, 無資格の

□ **inch** 名①インチ《長さの単位。1/12フィート, 2.54cm》②少量

□ **include** 動含む, 勘定に入れる

□ **including** 前～を含めて, 込みで

□ **income** 名収入, 所得, 収益

□ **incomplete** 形不完全な, 不十分な, 未完成の

□ **inconsistency** 名矛盾, 不一致

□ **incorrect** 形正しくない, 間違った

□ **increase** 動増加[増強]する, 増やす, 増える

□ **increased** 形増加した, 増大した

□ **increasingly** 副ますます, だんだん

□ **incredibly** 副信じられないほど, 途方もなく

□ **indeed** 副①実際, 本当に ②《強意》まったく

□ **independent** 形独立した, 自立

した

☐ **index** 名 ①索引 ②しるし, 現れ ③指標

☐ **index card** 索引カード

☐ **indicate** 動 ①指す, 示す, (道などを)教える ②それとなく言う ③きざしがある

☐ **indices** 名 index (指標)の複数形

☐ **indistinguishable** 形 区別ができない, 見分けがつかない

☐ **individual** 形 独立した, 個性的な, 個々の 名 個体, 個人

☐ **indoors** 副 室内で, 屋内で

☐ **induce** 動 (〜)する気持ちを起こさせる, 説得して〜させる

☐ **industrial** 形 工業の, 産業の

☐ **industry** 名 産業, 工業

☐ **inefficiency** 名 非能率, 能力不足

☐ **inevitable** 形 避けられない, 必然的な

☐ **infection** 名 (病気など)感染, 伝染

☐ **infestation** 名 (害虫・悪者・病気などの)まん延

☐ **inflammation** 名 ①炎症 ②激怒, 興奮

☐ **inflexible** 形 柔軟性のない, 融通の利かない

☐ **influence** 名 影響, 勢力 動 影響をおよぼす

☐ **initial** 形 最初の, 初めの

☐ **initialize** 動 初期化[イニシャライズ]する

☐ **innovation** 名 ①革新, 刷新 ②新しいもの, 新考案

☐ **innovative** 形 革新的な, 刷新的な

☐ **input** 動 入力する 名 入力データ, インプット

☐ **input layer** 入力層

☐ **insect** 名 虫, 昆虫

☐ **inspect** 動 検査する, 調べる

☐ **inspiration** 名 霊感, ひらめき, 妙案, 吸気

☐ **instant** 形 即時の, 緊急の, 即席の

☐ **instead** 副 その代わりに

☐ **institute** 名 協会, 研究所

☐ **institution** 名 ①設立, 制定 ②制度, 慣習 ③協会, 公共団体

☐ **institutional** 形 ①制度上の, 慣習上の ②協会の

☐ **instruct** 動 ①教える, 教育する ②指図[命令]する

☐ **instruction** 名 教えること, 指示, 助言

☐ **intake** 名 吸入(量), 摂取(量)

☐ **intellectual** 形 知的な, 知性のある

☐ **intelligence** 名 ①知能 ②情報

☐ **intelligence explosion** 知性爆発《「技術的特異点(シンギュラリティ)」に代わる新語》

☐ **intelligent** 形 頭のよい, 聡明な

☐ **intelligent agent** 知的エージェント《一種の人工知能的機能を有するソフトウェアエージェント。ユーザーを補助し, 繰り返し行うべきコンピューター関連のタスクをユーザーに代わって行うエージェントで, 学習し「適応」する能力を有する》

☐ **intelligently** 副 賢く, 知的に

☐ **intend** 動《-to 〜》〜しようと思う, 〜するつもりである

☐ **interact** 動 ①影響しあう, 相互に作用する ②心を通わせる

☐ **interaction** 名 相互作用, 相互の影響, 対話

☐ **interactive** 形 双方向(性)の, 対話式の, インタラクティブな

☐ **interested** 形 興味を持った, 関心のある **be interested in** 〜に興味[関心]がある

☐ **interesting** 形 おもしろい, 興味を起こさせる

☐ **interestingly** 副 面白い[興味深

い]ことに

□ **interface** 名 ①境界面 ②共通領域 ③インターフェース

□ **internal** 形 内部の，国内の，本質的な

□ **International Conference on Machine Learning** 機械学習に関する国際会議《機械学習と人工知能の研究に大きな影響を与える主要な会議の一つ》

□ **internationally** 副 国際的に

□ **Internet troll** インターネット・トロール《インターネット上での嫌がらせ行為。特に，ツイッターやフェースブックなどのソーシャルメディアで，悪意あるコメントをしつこく投稿したり，他人の話し合いを妨害したりすることを指す》

□ **interpretation** 名 ①解釈 ②通訳

□ **intersect** 動 (2本の道路・線などが)交差する，交わる

□ **intriguing** 形 興味をそそる，魅力的な

□ **introduction** 名 紹介，導入

□ **invasion** 名 侵略，侵害

□ **invent** 動 ①発明[考案]する ②ねつ造する

□ **invention** 名 ①発明(品) ②作り事，でっち上げ

□ **inventive** 形 発明の，発明の才のある，創意に富む

□ **inventor** 名 発明者，発案者

□ **invest** 動 投資する，(金・精力などを)注ぐ

□ **investment** 名 投資，出資

□ **investopedia.com** 名 インヴェストペディア《ニューヨーク市に本社を置く金融メディアWebサイト》

□ **investor** 名 ①出資者，投資家 ②授与者

□ **involve** 動 ①含む，伴う ②巻き込む，かかわらせる

□ **irreversible** 形 不可逆の

□ **Isaac Asimov** アイザック・アシモフ《アメリカ合衆国の作家・生化学者(ボストン大学教授)。特にSF，一般向け科学解説書，推理小説によってよく知られている。1920–1992》

□ **issue** 名 ①問題，論点 ②発行物 ③出口，流出

□ **It is ~ for someone to ...** (人)が…するのは～だ

□ **item** 名 ①項目，品目 ②(新聞などの)記事

□ **itself** 代 それ自体，それ自身

J

□ **Jacquard loom** ジャカード織機《1801年，ジョゼフ・マリー・ジャカールによって発明された自動織機》

□ **James Morgan** ジェームズ・N・モーガン《アメリカ合衆国の経済学者。1918–2018》

□ **Japan** 名 日本《国名》

□ **Japanese** 形 日本(人・語)の 名 ①日本人 ②日本語

□ **Jason Allen** ジェイソン・M・アレン《ゲームデザイナー，合成メディアアーティスト》

□ **Jenga** 名 ジェンガ《同サイズの直方体のパーツを組んで作ったタワーから崩さないように注意しながら片手で一片を抜き取り，最上段に積みあげる動作を交代で行うテーブルゲーム》

□ **Jeopardy!** 名『ジェパディ!』《アメリカ合衆国で放送されているクイズ番組。毎回3人の解答者(うち1名は前回放送時のチャンピオン)により対戦が行われ，クイズに正解することで獲得できる賞金の総額を競いあう》

□ **Jewish** 形 ユダヤ人の，ユダヤ教の

□ **John Basl** ジョン・バースル《哲学者，ノースイースタン大学教授》

□ **John Deere** ジョン・ディア《アメリカ合衆国イリノイ州に本社を置く農業機械、および建設機械のメーカー、ディア・アンド・カンパニー（Deere & Company）のブランド名》

□ **John Hopfield** ジョン・ホップフィールド《アメリカ合衆国の物理学者、生物学者。「連想型ニューラルネットワーク」の発明でよく知られており、これは現在ではホップフィールド・ネットワークと呼ばれている。1933–》

□ **John McCarthy** ジョン・マッカーシー《アメリカ合衆国の計算機科学者で認知科学者。LISPというプログラミング言語を開発。マービン・ミンスキーとならぶ初期の人工知能研究の第一人者。1927–2011》

□ **John Sonquist** ジョン・A・ソンクイスト《音楽家、編曲家、社会学者。1931–2017》

□ **John von Neumann** ジョン・フォン・ノイマン《ハンガリー出身のアメリカ合衆国の数学者。原子爆弾やコンピューターの開発への関与で知られる。1903–1957》

□ **joke** 名 冗談、ジョーク

□ **Joseph Hodges** ジョセフ・ローソン・ホッジス《アメリカ合衆国の統計家》

□ **Joseph Marie Jacquard** ジョゼフ・マリー・ジャカール《フランスの発明家。ジャカード織機というプログラム可能な初期の織機の開発で知られる。1752–1834》

□ **Joseph Weizenbaum** ジョセフ・ワイゼンバウム《ドイツ系アメリカ人でMITの計算機科学の名誉教授。1923–2008》

□ **journalism** 名 ジャーナリズム

□ **Joy Buolamwini** ジョイ・ブォロムウィニ《ガーナ系アメリカ人とカナダ人のコンピューター科学者であり、MITメディアラボを拠点とするデジタル活動家》

□ **judge** 動 判決を下す、裁く、判断する、評価する

□ **judgment** 名 ①判断、意見 ②裁判、判決

□ **justified** 形 理にかなった、もっともな

K

□ **Karel Čapek** カレル・チャペック《チェコの作家・劇作家・ジャーナリスト・園芸家。1890–1938》

□ **keep** 熟 **keep ~ in check** ~を抑制［制止・阻止・防止・けん制］する **keep ~ out of** ~を…から閉め出す **keep track of** ~の経過を追う

□ **kick off** 始める、キックオフする

□ **killer** 名 殺人者［犯］

□ **kind of** ある程度、いくらか、~のようなもの［人］

□ **k-nearest neighbors algorithm (KNN)** k近傍法《機械学習のアルゴリズムの一つ。最も簡単な機械学習のアルゴリズムの一つとされており、遅延学習に分類される》

□ **KNN** 略 k近傍法《機械学習のアルゴリズムの一つ。最も簡単な機械学習のアルゴリズムの一つとされており、遅延学習に分類される。k-nearest neighbors algorithmの略》

□ **knowledge** 名 知識、理解、学問

□ **known as** 《be –》~として知られている

□ **known to** 《be –》~に知られている

□ **Komodo** 名 Komodo《ドン・デイリーとチェス・グランドマスターのラリー・カウフマンによって作成されたエンジンを元にKomodo Chessが開発したUCIチェスエンジン》

□ **Korean** 形 韓国（人・語）の、朝鮮（人・語）の 名 ①韓国［朝鮮］人 ②韓国［朝鮮］語

□ **Kunihiko Fukushima** 福島 邦彦《日本の計算機科学者であり、ニュ

ーラルネットワークと深層学習の研究で有名。1936–》

L

□ **lab** 名研究室

□ **label** 名 ①ラベル, 名札 ②あだ名, レッテル

□ **label bias** ラベルバイアス《局所的に見て連接しやすいラベルを正解として選択しやすく, 結果的に全体でみると不自然な系列を選択してしまう現象》

□ **labeled data** ラベル付きデータ

□ **laboratory** 名実験室, 研究室

□ **lack** 動不足している, 欠けている 名不足, 欠乏

□ **laid** 動 lay (置く)の過去, 過去分詞

□ **LaMDA** 略ラムダ《高度な会話能力をもつGoogleの大規模言語モデル。Language Model for Dialogue Applicationsの略》

□ **lane** 名車線, 小道

□ **language** 熟 **natural language processing (NLP)** 自然言語処理《人間の言語(自然言語)を機械で処理し, 内容を抽出すること》 **universal language** 汎用言語

□ **Language Model for Dialogue Applications (LaMDA)** 対話アプリケーション用の言語モデル《高度な会話能力をもつGoogleの大規模言語モデル》

□ **largely** 副大いに, 主として

□ **lastly** 副最後に, 結局

□ **Latinx** 名〈米〉ラテンアメリカ系住民

□ **layer** 名層, 重ね **hidden layer** 隠れ層 **input layer** 入力層 **output layer** 出力層

□ **lazy** 形怠惰な, 無精な

□ **lazy (learner)** 怠惰学習, 遅延学習《教師データから何かしらの新しい方程式を作り出すのではなく, 単純に教師データを丸暗記するタイプの学習アルゴリズム》

□ **lead the way** 先に立って導く, 案内する, 率先する

□ **lead to** ～に至る, ～に通じる, ～を引き起こす

□ **leading** 形主要な, 指導的な, 先頭の

□ **leaf node** 葉ノード《子ノードを持たないノード。木構造の下位の末端にあるノード》

□ **league** 名 ①同盟, 連盟 ②(スポーツの)競技連盟

□ **league-based** 形リーグ制の

□ **leap** 熟 **by leaps and bounds** (進行・成長などが)急速に, 飛躍的に

□ **learning** 熟 **deep learning** ディープラーニング《十分なデータ量があれば, 人間の力なしに機械が自動的にデータから特徴を抽出してくれるディープニューラルネットワーク(DNN)を用いた学習のこと》 **multi-agent reinforcement learning** マルチエージェント強化学習《強化学習の一分野。シングルエージェント強化学習の研究が, 1つのエージェントにとって最大のポイント数を得るアルゴリズムを見つけることに関係しているのに対し, マルチエージェント強化学習の研究は, 協力, 互恵性, 公平性, 社会的影響力, 言語, 差別といった社会的指標を評価し定量化する》 **reinforcement learning** 強化学習《AIやコンピューターなどの「エージェント(学習者)」にデータを与えて学習させる「機械学習」の手法の一種》 **supervised learning** 教師あり学習《学習データに正解を与えた状態で学習させる手法》 **unsupervised learning** 教師なし学習《あえて正解が決まっていないデータをコンピューターに与え, AIが自律的に答えを判断できるよう学習させる手法》

□ **Learning from Delayed Rewards** 「Q学習」(Q-learning)という名前で近年流行りの機械学習

A B C D E F G H I J K **L** M N O P Q R S T U V W X Y Z

の手法をまとめたクリス・ワトキンズ（Chris Watkins）の論文。1989年

□ **least** 副いちばん小さく，最も少なく 名最小，最少 **at least** 少なくとも

□ **leave behind** あとにする，～を置き去りにする

□ **led** 動lead（導く）の過去，過去分詞

□ **Lee Luda** イルダ《韓国のベンチャー企業SCATTER LABが開発したチャットボット。愉快犯的なユーザーによる悪質な調教を受けたことでサービス停止》

□ **legal** 形法律（上）の，正当な

□ **legal move**（チェスなどにおける）合法手《ルール上可能な指し手》

□ **legend** 名伝説，伝説的人物，言い伝え

□ **length** 名長さ，縦，たけ，距離

□ **lens** 名レンズ

□ **Leonardo Torres Quevedo** レオナルド・トーレス・ケベード《スペイン人の技術者にして数学者。1852–1936》

□ **less** 形～より小さい［少ない］ 副～より少なく，～ほどでなく

□ **lethality** 名致死性，死亡率

□ **level** 名①水平，平面 ②水準 形①水平の，平たい ②同等［同位］の

□ **lever** 名てこ，レバー

□ **lie** 動（ある状態に）ある，存在する

□ **life** 熟**back to life** 生き返る，息を吹き返す

□ **life-imitation** 名生命模倣

□ **life-preservation** 名生命保存

□ **life-sized** 形等身大の

□ **light-skinned** 形肌が白い，色白の

□ **like** 熟**like this** このような，こんなふうに **look like** ～のように見える，～に似ている **sound like** ～のように聞こえる

□ **likely** 形①ありそうな，（～）しそうな ②適当な 副たぶん，おそらく

□ **likeness** 名（～に）よく似ていること

□ **limitation** 名制限，限度

□ **limit** 動（～を）限定［制限］する

□ **linear** 形①直線の，線状の ②一次元の

□ **list** 名名簿，目録，一覧表

□ **live-action** 形実写版の

□ **livestock** 名家畜

□ **living** 名生計，生活

□ **loan** 名貸付（金），ローン

□ **location** 名位置，場所

□ **logic** 名論理（学），理屈

□ **Logic Theorist (LT)** ロジック・セオリスト《1955年から1956年にかけてアレン・ニューウェル，ハーバート・サイモン，クリフォード・ショーが開発したコンピュータープログラム。「世界初の人工知能プログラム」と称された》

□ **logical** 形論理学の，論理的な

□ **long way** はるかに

□ **longer** 熟**no longer** もはや～でない［～しない］

□ **long-term** 形長期の

□ **look for** ～を探す

□ **look like** ～のように見える，～に似ている

□ **look up** 調べる

□ **loom** 名織り機

□ **loop** 名ループ，輪，輪状のもの 動輪を作る **loop back** 一巡して元に戻る

□ **loser** 名敗者

□ **loss** 名①損失（額・物），損害，浪費 ②失敗，敗北

□ **lover** 名①愛人，恋人 ②愛好者

□ **lower** 形もっと低い，下級の，劣った 動下げる，低くする

□ **low-level** 形低レベルの，下層の

□ **LT** 略 LT（ロジック・セオリスト）《1955年から1956年にかけてアレン・ニューウェル，ハーバート・サイモン，クリフォード・ショーが開発したコンピュータープログラム。「世界初の人工知能プログラム」と称された。Logic Theoristの略》

□ **LucasFilm** 名 ルーカスフィルム・リミテッド《ジョージ・ルーカスが設立した映像製作会社。2012年にウォルト・ディズニー・スタジオに約40億ドルで買収された》

□ **Ludwig van Beethoven** ルートヴィヒ・ヴァン・ベートーヴェン《ドイツの作曲家，ピアニスト。音楽史において極めて重要な作曲家の一人であり，日本では「楽聖」とも呼ばれる。1770–1827》

□ **Luke Skywalker** ルーク・スカイウォーカー《SF映画『スター・ウォーズ』シリーズ「エピソード4〜6」の主人公》

M

□ **machine learning (ML)** 機械学習《経験からの学習により自動で改善するコンピューターアルゴリズムもしくはその研究領域で，人工知能の一種であるとみなされている》

□ **machinery** 名 機械類［装置］

□ **macro** 名 マクロ

□ **MAD** 略 相互確証破壊《核戦略に関する概念・理論・戦略。核兵器を保有して対立する2か国のどちらか一方が，相手に対し先制的に核兵器を使用した場合，もう一方の国家は破壊を免れた核戦力によって確実に報復することを保証する。mutually assured destructionの略》

□ **MADALINE** 略 Multiple ADAptive LINear Elements《ADALINEユニットによる多層ネットワーク。ADALINEはパーセプトロンの数年後に発表されたパーセプトロンの改良版》

□ **made up of** 《be –》〜で構成されている

□ **magic** 名 ①魔法，手品 ②魔力

□ **main** 形 主な，主要な

□ **mainframe** 名 メインフレーム，大型汎用コンピューター

□ **maintain** 動 ①維持する ②養う

□ **major** 形 ①大きいほうの，主な，一流の ②年長［古参］の

□ **majority** 名 ①大多数，大部分 ②過半数

□ **make a trade** トレードする

□ **make sense** 意味をなす，よくわかる

□ **make up** 作り出す，考え出す，〜を構成［形成］する

□ **make use of** 〜を利用する，〜を生かす

□ **making** 名 制作，製造

□ **male** 名 男，雄

□ **manage** 動 ①動かす，うまく処理する ②経営［管理］する，支配する ③どうにか〜する

□ **management** 名 ①経営，取り扱い ②運営，管理（側）

□ **manager** 名 経営者，支配人，支店長，部長

□ **Mandalorian, The** 『マンダロリアン』《ルーカスフィルムが製作するアメリカ合衆国のインターネットテレビドラマシリーズ。2019–》

□ **manipulate** 動 操る，操作する，巧みに扱う

□ **manipulative** 形 思いどおりに操る（のがうまい），巧みに操作する

□ **manner** 名 ①方法，やり方 ②態度，様子 ③《-s》行儀，作法，生活様式

□ **manually** 副 手（作業）で

□ **manufacturer** 名 製造業者，メーカー

□ **manufacturing** 形 製造（業）の 名 製造（業）

□ **manuscript** 名 原稿，手書き原稿，写本

□ **map out** ～を緻密に計画する

□ **margin** 名 ①ふち，余白，欄外 ②余裕 ③利ざや，マージン

□ **Maria Theresa** マリア・テレジア《ハプスブルク帝国，いわゆるオーストリアの君主で実質的な「女帝」。1717–1780》

□ **mark** 動 ①印［記号］をつける ②採点する ③目立たせる

□ **Mark Hamill** マーク・ハミル《アメリカ合衆国の俳優，声優，作家。1951–》

□ **Mark Zuckerberg** マーク・ザッカーバーグ《アメリカ合衆国のプログラマー，実業家。Meta Platforms, Inc.（旧称：Facebook, Inc.）の共同創業者兼会長兼CEO。1984–》

□ **marker** 名 標識，印

□ **marketing** 名 マーケティング

□ **Markov chains** マルコフ連鎖《今現在からの状態が変化する確率が，これまでの状態がどのようなものであったかに関わらず，現在の状態のみから決定するようなモデルのこと》

□ **Marvin Minsky** マービン・ミンスキー《アメリカ合衆国のコンピューター科学者であり，認知科学者。専門は人工知能（AI）であり，「人工知能の父」と呼ばれる。1927–2016》

□ **Mary Shelley** メアリー・シェリー《イギリスの小説家。ゴシック小説『フランケンシュタイン』で知られる。1797–1851》

□ **master** 名 主人，雇い主，師，名匠 動 ①修得する ②～の主となる

□ **match** 名 ①試合，勝負 ②相手，釣り合うもの ③マッチ（棒） 動 ①～に匹敵する ②調和する，釣り合う ③（～を…と）勝負させる

□ **matchbox** 名 マッチ箱

□ **Matchbox Educable Noughts And Crosses Engine (MENACE)** Matchbox Educable Noughts And Crosses Engine《AIのはしりとなる機械学習型三目並べゲームエンジン。開発当初は全くコンピューターを使っておらず，マッチ箱を使って対戦経験により学習を行った》

□ **matching** 形 調和する

□ **mate-in-two problem** 2手メイト問題《チェスで，白が1手指し，黒がどのように応じても次の手で黒のキングが詰まされる問題》

□ **mathematical** 形 数学の，数理的な，正確な

□ **mathematician** 名 数学者

□ **mathematics** 名 数学

□ **Matrix, The** 『マトリックス』《アメリカのSFアクション映画，1999年》

□ **matter** 熟 **synthetic organic matter** 合成有機物

□ **Matthew Guzdial** マシュー・グズディアル《コンピューター科学者。アルバータ大学助教授》

□ **Max Planck Institute for Brain Research** マックス・プランク脳科学研究所《ドイツ連邦政府の公的資金により運営される研究機関の一つ》

□ **maximize** 動 ①最大にする ②最も広義に解釈する

□ **maximum** 形 最大限の，最高の

□ **means of** 《by –》～を用いて

□ **meanwhile** 副 それまでの間，一方では

□ **measure** 名 ①寸法，測定，計量，単位 ②程度，基準

□ **measurement** 名 測ること，計測，測定

□ **measurement bias** 測定バイアス《調査すべき変数に関して，対象者を不正確に測定（または分類）することによる系統的な誤差》

□ **mechanism** 名 機構，仕組み

□ **media** 名メデイア，マスコミ，媒体

□ **medical** 形 ①医学の ②内科の

□ **Megvii** 名 Megvii社《画像認識と深層学習ソフトウェアを設計する中国のテクノロジー企業。世界最大の第三者認証ソフトウェアのプロバイダー》

□ **meme** 名ミーム《遺伝子によらず，模倣によって人から人へと伝えられる情報の単位》**viral meme** バイラルミーム《インターネットを通じて人から人へと，通常は模倣として，ウイルスの感染のように拡がっていく行動・コンセプト・メディアのこと》

□ **memistor** 名メミスター《並列コンピューティングのメモリ技術に用いられるナノ電気回路素子》

□ **memory** 名 ①記憶（力），思い出 ②（コンピューターの）メモリ，記憶装置 **content-addressable memory** 連想メモリ《コンピューターなどの記憶装置（メモリ）の一種で，たいていの一般的なメモリは整数値などでアドレスを指定してその内容を読み書きするものであるのに対し，内容（の一部）を指定して，そのアドレスあるいは内容全体を読み出すことができる》

□ **MENACE** 略 MENACE《AIのはしりとなる機械学習型三目並べゲームエンジン。開発当初は全くコンピューターを使っておらず，マッチ箱を使って対戦経験により学習を行った。Matchbox Educable Noughts and Crosses Engineの略》

□ **Meno** 名『メノン』《プラトンの初期末の対話篇》

□ **mention** 動（〜について）述べる，言及する

□ **meow** 名ニャー，ニャオ《猫の鳴き声》

□ **Mephisto** 名メフィスト《1876年に作られたチェスをする「擬似オートマトン」。タークやアジーブとは異なり，隠れた操作者を持たず，代わりに電気機械的な手段で遠隔操作されていた》

□ **Mercedes-Benz** 名メルセデス《ドイツのダイムラー社製の高級乗用車》

□ **mere** 形単なる，ほんの，まったく〜にすぎない

□ **merely** 副単に，たかが〜に過ぎない

□ **Meta** 名メタ・プラットフォームズ《アメリカ合衆国のカリフォルニア州メンローパークに本社を置く多国籍テクノロジー・コングロマリット。旧称Facebook, Inc.》

□ **method** 名 ①方法，手段 ②秩序，体系

□ **Mexico** 名メキシコ《国名》

□ **mice** 名 mouse（ネズミ）の複数

□ **micro** 形極小の，ミクロの

□ **microchip** 名マイクロチップ

□ **Microsoft** マイクロソフト

□ **mid-** 形中間にある，中央の

□ **middle** 名中間，最中 **in the middle of** 〜の真ん中［中ほど］に 形中間の，中央の

□ **Midjourney** 名ミッドジャーニー《テキストの説明文から画像を作成する独自の人工知能プログラム》

□ **might** 助《mayの過去》①〜かもしれない ②〜してもよい，〜できる

□ **milestone** 名画期的出来事［事件］，節目

□ **military** 形軍隊［軍人］の，軍事の 名《the –》軍，軍部

□ **millennium** 名千年紀

□ **millisecond** 名1000分の1秒，ミリ秒

□ **mind** 名 ①心，精神，考え ②知性

□ **minimal** 形最小の，最低限の

□ **MiniMax theorem** ミニマックス定理《想定される最大の損害が最小になるように決断を行う戦略のこと。将棋，チェス，リバーシなどといった

完全情報ゲームをコンピューターに思考させるためのアルゴリズムとしても用いられる》

□ **minimize** 動最小にする，最小評価する

□ **minimum** 形最小(限)の，最低(限)の

□ **mirror** 名鏡

□ **misidentified** 形誤認された

□ **mistaken** 動mistake (間違える)の過去分詞

□ **MIT** 略マサチューセッツ工科大学

□ **mix** 名混合(物)

□ **mixed** 形①混合の，混ざった ②男女共学の

□ **ML** 略機械学習《経験からの学習により自動で改善するコンピューターアルゴリズムもしくはその研究領域で，人工知能の一種であるとみなされている。machine learningの略》

□ **model** 名①模型，設計図 ②模範 **classification model** 分類モデル《あるデータがどのクラスに属すかを判別するモデル》 **regression model** 回帰モデル《連続する値を入力し，将来や未知の事例についての予測をするモデル》 動(〜をもとにして)作る，模型を作る

□ **modern** 形現代[近代]の，現代的な，最近の

□ **Moderna** 名モデルナ《アメリカ合衆国マサチューセッツ州ケンブリッジに本社を置くバイオテクノロジー企業。メッセンジャーRNA(mRNA)のみに基づく創薬，医薬品開発，ワクチン技術に焦点を当てている》

□ **Mona Lisa** モナ・リザ《レオナルド・ダ・ビンチ作の肖像画》

□ **monitor** 動監視する，観察する

□ **monster** 名怪物

□ **moral** 形道徳(上)の，倫理的な，道徳的な

□ **morally** 副道徳的に，事実上

□ **more** 熟 **no more** もう〜ない

□ **mostly** 副主として，多くは，ほとんど

□ **moth** 名蛾，シミ，(衣類などの)虫食い

□ **motorist** 名自動車を運転する人

□ **mourner** 名会葬者

□ **move** 熟 **legal move** (チェスなどにおける)合法手《ルール上可能な指し手》 **move the goalposts** (特に秘密裏に)規則や条件を変える，後から決定を覆す **move to** 〜に移動する

□ **movement** 名①動き，運動 ②《-s》行動 ③引っ越し ④変動

□ **movie** 熟 **feature-length movie** 〈主に米〉長編映画

□ **moving** 形①動いている ②感動させる

□ **moving picture** 映画

□ **much** 熟 **as much as** 〜と同じだけ

□ **multi-agent** 形マルチエージェントの

□ **multi-agent reinforcement learning** マルチエージェント強化学習《強化学習の一分野。シングルエージェント強化学習の研究が，1つのエージェントにとって最大のポイント数を得るアルゴリズムを見つけることに関係しているのに対し，マルチエージェント強化学習の研究は，協力，互恵性，公平性，社会的影響力，言語，差別といった社会的指標を評価し定量化する》

□ **multibillion-dollar** 形数十億ドル(規模)の

□ **multilayered** 形重層化された，重層的な

□ **multiple** 形複合的な，多様な

□ **Multiple ADAptive LINear Elements (MADALINE)** ADALINEユニットによる多層ネットワーク。ADALINEはパーセプトロンの数年後に発表されたパーセプトロ

ンの改良版。

☐ **multisensory** 形 多感覚応用の

☐ **musician** 名 音楽家

☐ **musicologist** 名 音楽学者

☐ **mutually** 副 相互に, 互いに

☐ **mutually assured destruction (MAD)** 相互確証破壊《核戦略に関する概念・理論・戦略。核兵器を保有して対立する2か国のどちらか一方が, 相手に対し先制的に核兵器を使用した場合, もう一方の国家は破壊を免れた核戦力によって確実に報復することを保証する》

☐ **mysterious** 形 神秘的な, 謎めいた

☐ **mystery** 名 ①神秘, 不可思議 ②推理小説, ミステリー

☐ **mythology** 名 神話

N

☐ **naked mole rat** ハダカデバネズミ《アフリカのサバンナの地下に生息する, マウスと同程度の大きさの齧歯類》

☐ **nanobot** 名 ナノボット《ナノロボットのこと。細胞と同じほどの大きさの小さなロボット》

☐ **Napoleon Bonaparte** ナポレオン・ボナパルト《フランス革命期の軍人, 革命家で, フランス第一帝政の皇帝に即位してナポレオン1世となった。1769–1821》

☐ **narrow** 形 ①狭い ②限られた

☐ **narrow AI** 弱いAI《人間の知能の一部に特化した機能を実現するAIのこと。特化型AIも似たような意味で使われる。weak AIと同義》

☐ **National Institute of Standards and Technology (NIST)** アメリカ国立標準技術研究所《アメリカ合衆国の国立の計量標準研究所》

☐ **natural language processing (NLP)** 自然言語処理《人間の言語(自然言語)を機械で処理し, 内容を抽出すること》

☐ **natural language understanding (NLU)** 自然言語理解《人工知能の自然言語処理の一分野であり, コンピューターに自然言語を理解(読解)または意図を抽出させるという試み》

☐ **natural-language** 形 自然言語の

☐ **naturally** 副 生まれつき, 自然に, 当然

☐ **navigation** 名 航行, 航海, 操縦

☐ **navy** 名 海軍, 海軍力

☐ **nearest neighbor algorithm** 最近傍法《ニアレストネイバー法ともいう。新しいデータに対し, もっとも近い(数個の)既存データが属するクラスター(集団)に分類する》

☐ **near-future** 形 近未来の

☐ **nearly** 副 ①近くに, 親しく ②ほとんど, あやうく

☐ **necessary** 形 必要な, 必然の

☐ **necessity** 名 必要, 不可欠, 必要品

☐ **negotiation** 名 交渉, 話し合い

☐ **neighbor** 熟 **nearest neighbor algorithm** 最近傍法《ニアレストネイバー法ともいう。新しいデータに対し, もっとも近い(数個の)既存データが属するクラスター(集団)に分類する》

☐ **neither** 代 (2者のうち)どちらも〜でない **neither 〜 nor …** 〜も…もない

☐ **neocognitron** 名 ネオコグニトロン《1979年に福島邦彦によって提唱された畳み込みニューラルネットワーク》

☐ **Netherlands** 名 オランダ《国名》

☐ **network** 名 回路, 網状組織, ネットワーク **feed-forward neural**

network (**FNN**) 順伝播型ニューラルネットワーク《データがネットワークを構成する層の間を一方向(入力層から出力層へ)にしか流れない。前の層から次の層へと，順番に伝播していくネットワーク》**Hopfield network** ホップフィールド・ネットワーク《ニューラルネットワークの一モデル》**deep neural network** ディープニューラルネットワーク《ニューラルネットワークをディープラーニングに対応させて4層以上に層を深くしたもの》**neural network** ニューラルネットワーク《ニューラルネットワークとは，脳内の神経細胞(ニューロン)のネットワーク構造を模した数学モデルで，データから学習できるという特徴から，パターン認識，データ分類，未来の予測に活用されている》**Support-vector networks** Support-vector networks《コリーナ・コルテスとウラジミール・ヴァプニク共著による1995年の論文》**recurrent neural networks** 回帰型ニューラルネットワーク《内部に循環をもつニューラルネットワークの総称・クラス》

□ **neural** 形 神経の，神経系の

□ **neural network** ニューラルネットワーク《ニューラルネットワークとは，脳内の神経細胞(ニューロン)のネットワーク構造を模した数学モデルで，データから学習できるという特徴から，パターン認識，データ分類，未来の予測に活用されている》**deep neural network** ディープニューラルネットワーク《ニューラルネットワークをディープラーニングに対応させて4層以上に層を深くしたもの》**feed-forward neural network** (**FNN**) 順伝播型ニューラルネットワーク《データがネットワークを構成する層の間を一方向(入力層から出力層へ)にしか流れない。前の層から次の層へと，順番に伝播していくネットワーク》**recurrent neural networks** 回帰型ニューラルネットワーク《内部に循環をもつニューラルネットワークの総称・クラス》

□ **neuron** 名 ニューロン，神経単位

□ **neurophysiologist** 名 神経生理学者

□ **neuroscientist** 名 神経科学者

□ **nevertheless** 副 それにもかかわらず，それでもやはり

□ **New York Times, The** ニューヨーク・タイムズ

□ **news** 名 報道，ニュース，便り，知らせ

□ **newspaper** 名 新聞(紙)

□ **9/11** (米国で2001年9月11日に起こった)同時多発テロ事件

□ **Ninth Symphony** (ベートーヴェンの)第9交響曲

□ **NIST** 略 アメリカ国立標準技術研究所《アメリカ合衆国の国立の計量標準研究所。National Institute of Standards and Technologyの略》

□ **NLP** 略 自然言語処理《人間の言語(自然言語)を機械で処理し，内容を抽出すること。natural language processingの略》

□ **NLU** 略 自然言語理解《人工知能の自然言語処理の一分野であり，コンピューターに自然言語を理解(読解)または意図を抽出させるという試み。natural language understandingの略》

□ **no longer** もはや～でない[～しない]

□ **no more** もう～ない

□ **no one** 誰も[一人も]～ない

□ **nobody** 代 誰も[1人も]～ない

□ **node** 名 ノード《ネットワークへの接続ポイント》**leaf node** 葉ノード《子ノードを持たないノード。木構造の下位の末端にあるノード》**root node** ルートノード，根ノード《根ノードは木構造の最上位にあるノード》

□ **none** 代 (～の)何も[誰も・少しも]…ない

□ **non-female** 形 非女性の

☐ **non-Japanese** 形（日本人から見た）外国人の，日本人ではない人の

☐ **nonnumerical** 形（文字・データなどが）数字［数値］ではない

☐ **nonsense** 名ばかげたこと，ナンセンス

☐ **nor** 接～もまたない **neither～nor …** ～も…もない

☐ **norm** 名基準，規範

☐ **normal** 形普通の，平均の，標準的な

☐ **normally** 副普通は，通常は

☐ **North American Computer Chess Championship** 北米コンピューターチェス選手権

☐ **North Carolina** ノースカロライナ州

☐ **Northeastern University** ノースイースタン州立大学

☐ **not only ～ but (also) …** ～だけでなく…もまた

☐ **not yet** まだ～してない

☐ **not ～ at all** 少しも［全然］～ない

☐ **not ～ but …** ～ではなくて…

☐ **note** 名①メモ，覚え書き ②注釈 ③注意，注目 ④手形 動①書き留める ②注意［注目］する

☐ **notice** 名①注意 ②通知 ③公告 動①気づく，認める ②通告する

☐ **notify** 動知らせる，通知する，報告する，届け出る

☐ **noughts and crosses** 三目並べ《3×3の格子を用意し，二人が交互に「○」と「×」を書き込んでいき3つ並べるゲーム。米国名はtic-tac-toe》

☐ **novel** 名（長編）小説

☐ **nuclear** 形核の，原子力の

☐ **nuclear-armed** 形核装備の，核武装の［した］

☐ **number of** 《a－》いくつかの～，多くの～

☐ **numeric** 形数字［数値］の［に関する］

O

☐ **Obama** 名バラク・フセイン・オバマ2世《アメリカ合衆国の政治家，弁護士。同国第44代大統領。1961–》

☐ **object** 名①物，事物 ②目的物，対象 動反対する，異議を唱える

☐ **observe** 動①観察［観測］する，監視［注視］する ②気づく ③守る，遵守する

☐ **observer** 名観察者，オブザーバー

☐ **obsolete** 形時代遅れの，すたれた

☐ **obstacle** 名障害（物），じゃま（な物）

☐ **occasion** 名①場合，（特定の）時 ②機会，好機 ③理由，根拠

☐ **occur** 動（事が）起こる，生じる，（考えなどが）浮かぶ

☐ **of course** もちろん，当然

☐ **of the time** 当時の，当節の

☐ **of which** ～の中で

☐ **off** 熟 **kick off** 始める，キックオフする **turn off** ①興味を失う，～にうんざりする ②～を止める，（照明などを）消す ③（道から）それる，（道が）～から分かれる

☐ **offensive** 形①いやな，いらいらさせる ②攻撃的な

☐ **offer** 動申し出る，申し込む，提供する

☐ **officer** 名役人，公務員，警察官

☐ **offline** 名《通信》オフライン，非直結

☐ **oil** 名①油，石油 ②油絵の具，油絵

☐ **old-fashioned** 形時代遅れの，旧式な

☐ **on the other hand** 一方，他方では

☐ **on the rise** 増加している

☐ **oncology** 名腫瘍学

☐ **oncology expert** 《病理》がん［腫瘍］専門医

□ **one** 熟 **each one** 各自 **no one** 誰も［一人も］～ない **one another** お互い **one by one** 1つずつ，1人ずつ

□ **online** 名 オンライン 形 オンラインの，ネットワーク上の

□ **only** 熟 **not only ～ but (also) …** ～だけでなく…もまた

□ **onto** 前 ～の上へ［に］

□ **ontology** 名 オントロジー，概念（化）の明示的仕様

□ **open up** 広がる，広げる，開く，開ける

□ **OpenAI** OpenAI（オープンエーアイ）《営利法人OpenAI LPとその親会社である非営利法人OpenAI Inc.からなる人工知能（AI）研究所》

□ **open-ended** 形（回答形式が）自由な，フリーアンサーの

□ **open-source** 形 オープンソースの

□ **opera** 名 歌劇，オペラ

□ **operate** 動 ①（機械などが）動く，運転する，管理する，操業する ②作用する ③手術する

□ **operation** 名 ①操作，作業，動作 ②経営，運営 ③手術 ④作戦，軍事行動

□ **operator** 名 オペレーター，交換手，操作する人

□ **opponent** 名 競争相手，敵，反対者

□ **opportunity** 名 好機，適当な時期［状況］

□ **optical** 形 眼の，光学（上）の

□ **optimal** 形 最適な，最善の

□ **optimization** 名 最適化

□ **optimization problem** 最適化問題《与えられた制約条件の下で，ある目的関数を大または最小にする解を求めること》

□ **option** 名 選択（の余地），選択可能物，選択権

□ **order** 熟 **in order to** ～するために，～しようと

□ **ordinary** 形 ①普通の，通常の ②並の，平凡な

□ **organic** 形 ①有機（化学）の ②臓器の ③有機農法の，化学肥料を用いない **synthetic organic matter** 合成有機物

□ **organization** 名 ①組織（化），編成，団体，機関 ②有機体，生物

□ **organize** 動 組織する

□ **organized** 動 organize（組織する）の過去，過去分詞 形 組織化された，よくまとまった

□ **original** 形 ①始めの，元の，本来の ②独創的な

□ **other** 熟 **each other** お互いに **every other** 1つおきの～，他のすべての **in other words** すなわち，言い換えれば **on the other hand** 一方，他方では

□ **otherwise** 副 さもないと，そうでなければ

□ **out** 熟 **carry out**［計画を］実行する **figure out** 理解する，～であるとわかる，（原因などを）解明する **find out** 見つけ出す，気がつく，知る，調べる，解明する **help out with** ～を手伝う **keep ～ out of** ～を…から閉め出す **out of** ①～から外へ，～から抜け出して ②～から作り出して，～を材料として ③～の範囲外に，～から離れて ④（ある数）の中から **out of control** コントロールできない，手に負えない **turn out to be** ～という結果になる **work out** うまくいく，何とかなる，（問題を）解く，考え出す，答えが出る，～の結果になる

□ **outcome** 名 結果，結末

□ **outlet** 名 ①出口 ②（電気の）コンセント

□ **out-of-control** 形 制御不能の［に陥った］

□ **outperform** 動（～を）しのぐ，上回る

□ **output** 名 アウトプット，出力

□ **output layer** 出力層

□ **over** 熟 **all over the world** 世界中に **over and over** 何度も繰り返して **over time** 時間とともに，そのうち **take over** 引き継ぐ，支配する，乗っ取る

□ **overall** 形 総体的な，全面的な

□ **overcast** 動 曇る

□ **overhead** 形 頭上に，真上に

□ **overlook** 動 ①見落とす，(チャンスなどを)逃す ②見渡す ③大目に見る

□ **overreact** 動 過剰反応する

□ **owner** 名 持ち主，オーナー

□ **oxygen** 名 酸素

P

□ **paid** 動 pay (払う)の過去，過去分詞

□ **pair** 名 (2つから成る)一対，一組，ペア

□ **paragraph** 名 段落，パラグラフ

□ **parameter** 名 (プログラムを呼び出すときの)引数，パラメーター

□ **parent** 名《-s》両親

□ **partial** 形 ①一部分の，不公平な ②特に好きな

□ **participant** 名 参加者，出場者，関与者

□ **participation** 名 参加，関与

□ **particular** 形 ①特別の ②詳細な

□ **particularly** 副 特に，とりわけ

□ **pass away** 過ぎ去る，終わる，死ぬ

□ **pass by** ～のそばを通る［通り過ぎる］

□ **pass through** ～を通る，通行する

□ **passenger** 名 乗客，旅客

□ **past** 形 過去の，この前の 名 過去(の出来事)

□ **pathway** 名 小道，通路

□ **patient** 名 病人，患者

□ **pattern** 名 ①柄，型，模様 ②手本，模範

□ **pay** 動 ①支払う，払う，報いる，償う ②割に合う，ペイする

□ **payload** 名 ペイロード《伝送されるパケットのヘッダー部を除いたデータの本体》

□ **payment** 名 支払い，払い込み

□ **pedestrian** 名 歩行者，通行人

□ **penny** 名 ①ペニー，ペンス《英国の貨幣単位。1/100ポンド》 ②《否定文で》小銭，びた一文

□ **penny challenge** ペニーチャレンジ《コンセントに充電器のプラグを半分ほど挿した状態でプラグに硬貨を落下させるというもの。硬貨が充電器のプラグに接触すると大電流が流れ，火花が出る》

□ **per** 前 ～につき，～ごとに

□ **perceive** 動 気づく，感知する

□ **perception** 名 認識，知覚(力)，認知，理解(力) **visual perception** 視覚

□ **Perceptron** 名 パーセプトロン《人工ニューロンやニューラルネットワークの一種。フランク・ローゼンブラットが1957年に考案》

□ **perform** 動 ①(任務などを)行う，果たす，実行する ②演じる，演奏する

□ **performance** 名 ①実行，行為 ②成績，できばえ，業績 ③演劇，演奏，見世物

□ **perhaps** 副 たぶん，ことによると

□ **period** 名 ①期，期間，時代 ②ピリオド，終わり

□ **permission** 名 許可，免許

□ **persona** 名 (劇などの)登場人物，ペルソナ，外的人格

□ **personal** 形 ①個人の, 私的な ②本人自らの **virtual personal assistant** 仮想パーソナルアシスタント《個人のタスクまたはサービスを実行できるソフトウェアエージェント》

□ **personality** 名 人格, 個性

□ **personalized** 形 パーソナライズされた

□ **Peter Norvig** ピーター・ノーヴィグ《アメリカ合衆国の計算機科学者。ACMおよびAAAIのフェロー, Google研究本部長》

□ **Pfizer** 名 ファイザー《アメリカ合衆国ニューヨーク州に本社を置く大手製薬会社》

□ **pH** 名 ペーハー, ピーエイチ

□ **Ph.D.** 略 博士号

□ **phantom** 形 実体のない, 錯覚の, 実在しない

□ **phantom braking** ファントムブレーキ《主にオートパイロット使用時に見られる誤認緊急停止。なんの前触れもなく勝手に自動で緊急ブレーキがかかること》

□ **pharmaceutical** 形 薬剤の, 薬局の

□ **phase** 名 ①段階, 局面 ②側面, 様相

□ **philosopher** 名 哲学者, 賢者

□ **philosophy** 名 哲学, 主義, 信条, 人生観

□ **photo** 名 写真

□ **phrase** 名 句, 慣用句, 名言

□ **physical** 形 ①物質の, 物理学の, 自然科学の ②身体の, 肉体の

□ **physics** 名 物理学

□ **picnic** 名 ピクニック

□ **pixel** 名 ピクセル, 画素

□ **place** 熟 **take place** 行われる, 起こる

□ **platform** 名 プラットホーム, 壇

□ **Plato** 名 プラトン《古代ギリシアの哲学者。紀元前427–紀元前347》

□ **play against** ～を相手にする

□ **player** 名 ①競技者, 選手, 演奏者, 俳優 ②演奏装置

□ **playwright** 名 脚本家, 劇作家

□ **plea** 名 嘆願

□ **plenty** 名 十分, たくさん, 豊富 **plenty of** たくさんの～

□ **plow** 動 すく, 耕す

□ **plug** 動 栓をする, ふさぐ **plug in** (～を) コンセントにつなぐ

□ **poetry** 名 詩歌, 詩を書くこと

□ **Pokémon** 名 ポケットモンスター《ゲーム》

□ **poker** 名 ①(トランプで) ポーカー ②火かき棒

□ **poker-playing** 形 ポーカーをプレイする

□ **policy** 名 ①政策, 方針, 手段 ②保険証券

□ **political** 形 ①政治の, 政党の ②策略的な

□ **politician** 名 政治家, 政略家

□ **pop up** (不意に) 現れる, 出現する

□ **population** 名 人口, 住民(数)

□ **pornography** 名 ポルノ(グラフィー)

□ **portal** 名 ポータル

□ **portfolio** 名 (個人や会社の保有する全ての) 有価証券(一覧), ポートフォリオ

□ **pose** 動 ①ポーズをとる[とらせる] ②気取る, 見せかける ③引き起こす

□ **position** 名 ①位置, 場所, 姿勢 ②地位, 身分, 職 ③立場, 状況

□ **positive** 名 ①正数, プラス, 陽極 ②ポジ, 陽画

□ **possible** 形 ①可能な ②ありうる, 起こりうる

□ **possibly** 副 ①あるいは, たぶん

②《否定文，疑問文で》どうしても，できる限り，とても，なんとか

□ **potential** 形可能性がある，潜在的な 名可能性，潜在能力

□ **pour** 動 ①注ぐ，浴びせる ②流れ出る，流れ込む ③ざあざあ降る

□ **poverty** 名貧乏，貧困，欠乏，不足

□ **powerful** 形力強い，実力のある，影響力のある

□ **practical** 形 ①実際的な，実用的な，役に立つ ②経験を積んだ

□ **prairie** 名大草原，プレーリー

□ **precious** 形 ①貴重な，高価な ②かわいい，大事な

□ **precise** 形正確な，ち密な，ぴったりした

□ **predator** 名捕食［肉食］動物

□ **predecessor** 名前任者，先祖

□ **predict** 動予測［予想］する

□ **prediction** 名予言，予報，予測

□ **predictive** 形予言する，予報する

□ **predictive text** 入力予測《コンピューターで文字を入力する際，入力したい語をソフトウェアが予測・提示する機能》

□ **prefer** 動（～のほうを）好む，（～のほうが）よいと思う

□ **preferable** 形選ぶに値する，望ましい

□ **prejudice** 名偏見，先入観

□ **prejudice bias** 偏見

□ **premiere** 動（映画が）封切られる

□ **pre-process** 動前［予備的］処理をする

□ **pre-programmed** 形前もってプログラムされた

□ **prescribe** 動 ①指図する，規定する ②（薬を）処方する

□ **presence** 名 ①存在すること ②出席，態度

□ **presently** 副 ①やがて，じき ②今，目下

□ **preservation** 名保護，保守

□ **preserve** 動保存［保護］する，保つ

□ **president** 名 ①大統領 ②社長，学長，頭取

□ **presidential** 形大統領の

□ **pressure** 名プレッシャー，圧力，圧縮，重荷

□ **pre-trained** 形事前に訓練された

□ **prevent** 動 ①妨げる，じゃまする ②予防する，守る，《－～ from …》～が…できない［しない］ようにする

□ **previous** 形前の，先の

□ **previously** 副あらかじめ，以前に［は］

□ **prewritten** 形事前に［前もって］書いた

□ **price** 名 ①値段，代価 ②《-s》物価，相場

□ **primarily** 副第一に，最初に，根本的に

□ **primary** 形第一の，主要な，最初の，初期の

□ **Principia Mathematica** 『プリンキピア・マテマティカ』《『数学原理』とも訳される，数学の基礎に関する著作。アルフレッド・ノース・ホワイトヘッドとバートランド・ラッセルの共著》

□ **prioritize** 動（～を）優先する［させる］

□ **privacy** 名（干渉されない）自由な生活，プライバシー

□ **pro** 名プロ（の選手），玄人，専門家

□ **probability** 名見込み，可能性

□ **probability theory** 確率論

□ **probable** 形ありそうな，有望な

□ **probably** 副たぶん，あるいは

□ **problem** 熟 **mate-in-two problem** 2手メイト問題《チェスで，白が1手指し，黒がどのように応

じても次の手で黒のキングが詰まされる問題》**traveling salesman problem (TSP)** 巡回セールスマン問題《セールスマンが所定の複数の都市を1回だけ巡回する場合の最短経路を求める組合せ最適化問題》**trolley problem** トロッコ問題《「ある人を助けるために他の人を犠牲にするのは許されるか？」という形で功利主義と義務論の対立を扱った倫理学上の問題・課題》

□ **procedure** 名 手順, 手続き

□ **proceed** 動 進む, 進展する, 続ける

□ **process** 名 ①過程, 経過, 進行 ②手順, 方法, 製法, 加工

□ **processing** 熟 **natural language processing (NLP)** 自然言語処理《人間の言語(自然言語)を機械で処理し, 内容を抽出すること》

□ **processor** 名 ①処理装置, プロセッサー ②加工[処理]業者

□ **product** 名 ①製品, 産物 ②成果, 結果

□ **production** 名 製造, 生産

□ **professional** 形 専門の, プロの, 職業的な

□ **professor** 名 教授, 師匠

□ **profit** 名 利益, 利潤, ため

□ **profound** 形 深い, 深遠な, 心の底から, 難解な

□ **program** 動 プログラミングする

□ **programmer** 名 プログラマー

□ **programming** 名 プログラミング

□ **progress** 名 ①進歩, 前進 ②成り行き, 経過

□ **project** 名 ①計画, プロジェクト ②研究課題

□ **promising** 形 有望な, 見込みのある

□ **promote** 動 促進する, 昇進[昇級]させる

□ **promotion** 名 ①昇進 ②促進 ③宣伝販売

□ **prompt** 名 ①促進 ②(演劇での)せりふづけ, 後見 ③(コンピューターの)プロンプト

□ **prong** 名 (フォークなどの)とがった先, また.

□ **propose** 動 ①申し込む, 提案する ②結婚を申し込む

□ **protein** 名 タンパク質, プロテイン

□ **prove** 動 ①証明する ②(～であることが)わかる, (～と)なる

□ **provide** 動 ①供給する, 用意する, (～に)備える ②規定する

□ **provoke** 動 ①怒らせる ②刺激して～させる ③引き起こす

□ **proximal** 形 隣接した, 近接した

□ **psychologist** 名 心理学者, 精神分析医

□ **public** 名 一般の人々, 大衆 形 公の, 公開の

□ **public domain** パブリックドメイン《著作物や発明などの知的創作物について, 知的財産権が発生していない状態または消滅した状態のこと》

□ **publish** 動 ①発表[公表]する ②出版[発行]する

□ **punch** 動 げんこつでなぐる

□ **punch card** パンチカード《厚手の紙に穴を開けて, その位置や有無から情報を記録する記録媒体》

□ **purpose-built** 形 専用の

□ **put in** ～の中に入れる

Q

□ **Q-learning** 名 Q学習《機械学習分野における強化学習の一種》

□ **quality** 名 ①質, 性質, 品質 ②特性 ③良質

□ **quantify** 動 (～を)数値化[数量化・定量化]する

A B C D E F G H I J K L M N O P Q R S T U V W X Y Z

□ **quantity** 名 ①量 ②《-ties》多量, たくさん

□ **queen** 名 女王, 王妃

□ **query** 名 クエリー《データベースへの検索要求。ソフトウェアに対するデータの問い合わせや要求などを一定の形式で文字に表現すること》

□ **quickly** 副 敏速に, 急いで

□ **quiz** 名 クイズ, テスト, 試験

R

□ **racism** 名 人種差別 **systemic racism** 制度的人種差別

□ **radical** 形 急進的な, 過激な

□ **radiologist** 名 放射線科医(師)

□ **radiology** 名 放射線(医)学

□ **railway** 名 鉄道

□ **raise** 動 ①上げる, 高める ②起こす ③〜を育てる ④(資金を)調達する

□ **random** 形 手当たり次第の, 無作為の

□ **random (decision) forest** ランダムフォレスト《複数の決定木を組み合わせ, 汎化能力を高めた頑健で実用的なアルゴリズム》

□ **range** 名 列, 連なり, 範囲

□ **rapid** 形 速い, 急な, すばやい

□ **rapidly** 副 速く, 急速, すばやく, 迅速に

□ **rat** 名 ネズミ

□ **rate** 名 ①割合, 率 ②相場, 料金 動 ①見積もる, 評価する[される] ②等級をつける

□ **rather** 副 ①むしろ, かえって ②かなり, いくぶん, やや ③それどころか逆に **rather than** 〜よりむしろ

□ **rating** 名 格付け, 評価, 採点

□ **rational** 形 理性的な, 合理的な

□ **rational agent** 合理的エージェント《エージェントが置かれている.環境で最良の結果を達成するために行動するエージェント》

□ **rational thought** 理性的思考

□ **rationality** 名 合理性, 理性のあること

□ **raw** 形 ①生の, 未加工の ②未熟な

□ **raw data** 加工されていないデータ, 未加工データ, 生データ, 原資料

□ **reader** 名 ①読者 ②読本, リーダー

□ **ready to** 《be –》すぐに[いつでも]〜できる, 〜する構えで

□ **real estate** 不動産, 土地

□ **realistic** 形 現実的な, 現実主義の

□ **reality** 名 現実, 実在, 真実(性)

□ **realize** 動 理解する, 実現する

□ **real-time strategy (RTS)** リアルタイムストラテジー《コンピューターゲームのジャンルの一つ。プレイヤーはリアルタイムに進行する時間に対応しつつ, プランを立てながら敵と戦う》

□ **real-world** 形 現実の世界の, 実在の

□ **reasonable** 形 筋の通った, 分別のある

□ **reasoning** 形 推論

□ **recently** 副 近ごろ, 最近

□ **recipe** 名 調理法, レシピ

□ **recognition** 名 識別, 認識 **facial recognition** 顔認識 **speech recognition** 音声認識, 言語認識

□ **recognize** 動 認める, 認識[承認]する

□ **recommendation** 名 ①推薦(状) ②勧告

□ **record** 名 ①記録, 登録, 履歴 ②(音楽などの)レコード 動 ①記録[登録]する ②録音[録画]する

□ **recording** 名 録音, 録画, レコーディング

□ **recruit** 動（人材を）募集する，勧誘する

□ **recurrent** 形 回帰性の

□ **recurrent neural networks (RNN)** 回帰型ニューラルネットワーク《内部に循環をもつニューラルネットワークの総称・クラス》

□ **reduce** 動 ①減じる ②しいて～させる，（～の）状態にする

□ **reduction** 名 ①下げること，減少，値下げ，割引 ②縮図 ③換算，約分，還元 **dimensionality reduction** 次元削減《高次元空間から低次元空間へデータを変換しながら，低次元表現が元データの何らかの意味ある特性を保持すること》

□ **refer** 動 ①《－to ～》～に言及する，～を指す ②～を参照する，～に問い合わせる

□ **reference** 名 言及，参照，照会

□ **refine** 動 純化する，精錬［精製］する，洗練する

□ **reflect** 動 映る，反響する，反射する

□ **regard** 動 ①（～を…と）見なす ②尊敬する，重きを置く ③関係がある

□ **regarding** 前 ～に関しては，～について

□ **regardless** 副 それにもかかわらず，それでも

□ **register** 動 登録する，署名する，書留にする

□ **regression** 名 回帰

□ **regression model** 回帰モデル《連続する値を入力し，将来や未知の事例についての予測をするモデル》

□ **regression tree** 回帰木《連続して変わりうる値を分析する場合に用いられる》

□ **regular** 形 ①規則的な，秩序のある ②定期的な，一定の，習慣的

□ **regularly** 副 整然と，規則的に

□ **reinforcement** 名 補強，強化

□ **reinforcement learning** 強化学習《AIやコンピューターなどの「エージェント（学習者）」にデータを与えて学習させる「機械学習」の手法の一種》 **multi-agent reinforcement learning** マルチエージェント強化学習《強化学習の一分野。シングルエージェント強化学習の研究が，1つのエージェントにとって最大のポイント数を得るアルゴリズムを見つけることに関係しているのに対し，マルチエージェント強化学習の研究は，協力，互恵性，公平性，社会的影響力，言語，差別といった社会的指標を評価し定量化する》

□ **related** 形 ①関係のある，関連した ②姻戚の

□ **relation** 名 ①（利害）関係，間柄 ②親戚

□ **relationship** 名 関係，関連，血縁関係

□ **relative** 形 関係のある，相対的な

□ **relatively** 副 比較的，相対的に

□ **release** 動 ①解き放す，釈放する ②免除する ③発表する，リリースする

□ **reliable** 形 信頼できる，確かな

□ **reliably** 副 確実に

□ **religion** 名 宗教，～教，信条

□ **rely** 動（人が…に）頼る，当てにする

□ **remain** 動 ①残っている，残る ②（～の）ままである［いる］

□ **remark** 名 ①注意，注目，観察 ②意見，記事，批評 動 ①注目する ②述べる，批評する

□ **rematch** 名 再試合

□ **remove** 動 ①取り去る，除去する ②（衣類を）脱ぐ

□ **repeat** 動 繰り返す

□ **rephrase** 動 言い直す，言い換える

□ **replace** 動 ①取り替える，差し替える ②元に戻す

□ **reply** 名答え, 返事, 応答

□ **reportedly** 副伝えられるところによると

□ **represent** 動 ①表現する ②意味する ③代表する

□ **representative** 名 ①代表(者), 代理人 ②代議士 ③典型, 見本

□ **reproduce** 動 ①再生する, 再現する ②複写する, 模造する

□ **request** 名願い, 要求(物), 需要

□ **require** 動 ①必要とする, 要する ②命じる, 請求する

□ **requirement** 名必要なもの, 必要条件

□ **research** 名調査, 研究 **research and development** 研究開発

□ **researcher** 名調査員, 研究者

□ **resident** 名居住者, 在住者

□ **resign** 動辞職する, やめる, 断念する

□ **resistor** 名レジスタ, 抵抗(器)

□ **resolve** 動決心する, 解決する

□ **respond** 動答える, 返答[応答]する

□ **response** 名応答, 反応, 返答

□ **responsible** 形責任のある, 信頼できる, 確実な

□ **restrict** 動制限する, 禁止する

□ **result** 名結果, 成り行き, 成績 動(結果として)起こる, 生じる, 結局〜になる

□ **resume** 動再び始める, 再開する

□ **retaliation** 名報復

□ **retreat** 名避難, 引退

□ **reveal** 動明らかにする, 暴露する, もらす

□ **revenue** 名所得, 収入, 利益, (国の)歳入

□ **review** 名 ①書評, 評論 ②再調査 ③復習 動 ①批評する ②再調査する ③復習する

□ **revise** 動 ①改訂[改正]する ②復習する

□ **revolt** 動そむく, 反乱を起こす

□ **revolution** 名 ①革命, 変革 ②回転, 旋回

□ **revolutionary** 形革命の, 画期的な, 革命的な

□ **reward** 名報酬, 償い, 応報

□ **rewrite** 動書き直す

□ **Richard Nixon** リチャード・ニクソン《アメリカ合衆国の政治家, 同国第37代大統領。1913–1994》

□ **rise** 熟 on the rise 増加している

□ **risk** 名危険

□ **RNN** 略回帰型ニューラルネットワーク《内部に循環をもつニューラルネットワークの総称・クラス。recurrent neural networksの略》

□ **robe** 名 ①ローブ, 化粧着, 部屋着 ②《-s》式服, 法衣

□ **robot** 名ロボット

□ **robotic** 形ロボットの[のような・による・を利用した]

□ **robust** 形(システムが)安定している, 堅固な

□ **robustness** 名頑健性, 構造安定性

□ **role** 名 ①(劇などの)役 ②役割, 任務

□ **room-size** 形部屋の大きさほどの

□ **root** 名 ①根, 根元 ②根源, 原因 ③《-s》先祖, ルーツ

□ **root node** ルートノード, 根ノード《根ノードは木構造の最上位にあるノード》

□ **Rossum's Universal Robots** 『R.U.R.』《「ロッサム万能ロボット会社」。チェコの作家カレル・チャペックにより1920年に発表された戯曲》

□ **rotor** 名回転翼, ローター

□ **route** 名道, 道筋, 進路, 回路
□ **routine** 名お決まりの手順, 日課
□ **RTS** 略リアルタイムストラテジー《コンピューターゲームのジャンルの一つ。プレイヤーはリアルタイムに進行する時間に対応しつつ, プランを立てながら敵と戦う。real-time strategy の略》
□ **rude** 形粗野な, 無作法な, 失礼な
□ **rule-based** 形規則［規定・ルール］に基づく
□ **run on** ～で動作する
□ **Russian** 名ロシア（人・語）の 名①ロシア人 ②ロシア語
□ **Rutgers University** ラトガーズ大学

S

□ **sadly** 副悲しそうに, 不幸にも
□ **SAE** 略米国自動車技術者協会《モビリティ専門家を会員とする米国の非営利団体。Society of Automotive Engineersの略》
□ **safety** 名安全, 無事, 確実
□ **safety-critical** 形セーフティクリティカルな, 安全が重大な結果に関わる
□ **sale** 名販売, 取引, 大売り出し
□ **sales** 形販売の
□ **salesman** 名男子販売員, セールスマン **traveling salesman problem (TSP)** 巡回セールスマン問題《セールスマンが所定の複数の都市を1回だけ巡回する場合の最短経路を求める組合せ最適化問題》
□ **salon** 名①（美容関係の）店 ②客間, サロン
□ **same ~ as ...** 《the –》…と同じ（ような）～
□ **same goes for** 《the –》～についても同じことが言える
□ **sample** 名サンプル,（抽出）標本
□ **sample bias** サンプリングバイアス《不適切な標本抽出によって, 母集団を代表しない特定の性質のデータが紛れ込んでいること》
□ **Samuel Checkers-Playing Program** Samuel Checkers-playing Program《世界初の学習型プログラムであり, 人工知能（AI）の基本的概念をいち早く世界に示したもの》
□ **San Francisco** サンフランシスコ《米国の都市》
□ **satisfy** 動①満足させる, 納得させる ②（義務を）果たす, 償う
□ **saturation** 名飽和（状態）
□ **scare** 動こわがらせる, おびえる
□ **schedule** 動予定を立てる
□ **schoolchildren** 名schoolchild（学童）の複数
□ **score** 名（競技の）得点, スコア,（試験の）点数, 成績
□ **scream** 動叫ぶ, 金切り声を出す
□ **screen** 名仕切り, 幕, スクリーン, 画面
□ **script** 名台本, スクリプト, 手書き
□ **SDQ** 略SDQ《AIを用いたデータ出力要求。複雑で手間のかかる臨床データ解析を効率化させた。Smart Data Queryの略》
□ **search** 動捜し求める, 調べる 名捜査, 探索, 調査
□ **search tree** 探索木《計算機科学において特定のキーを特定するために使用される木構造》
□ **seat** 動座らせる, 据え付ける
□ **secure** 動①安全にする ②確保する, 手に入れる
□ **security** 名①安全（性）, 安心 ②担保, 抵当,《-ties》有価証券
□ **Se-dol Lee** 李 世乭（イ・セドル）《韓国の元囲碁棋士。李昌鎬に次ぐ国際棋戦の優勝数回を誇り, 2000年代

半ばから2010年代前半における世界最強の棋士と目されている》

□ **seem** 動（～に）見える，（～のように）思われる

□ **select** 動 選択する，選ぶ

□ **selection** 名 選択（物），選抜，抜粋

□ **self-aware** 形 自我［自己認識］を持つ

□ **self-driving** 形（車などが）自動運転の

□ **self-governing** 形（国・組織などが）自治の

□ **self-learning** 形 自己学習型の

□ **self-supervised** 形 自己管理下の，自分で指揮［監督］する

□ **semi-supervised** 形 半教師付きの

□ **sense** 名 ①感覚，感じ ②《-s》意識，正気，本性 ③常識，分別，センス ④意味 **make sense** 意味をなす，よくわかる

□ **sensor** 名 センサー，感知装置

□ **sensory** 形 知覚の，感覚の

□ **sentence** 名 文

□ **sentient** 形（人工知能などが）意識［（人間のような）知覚］を持つ

□ **separate** 動 ①分ける，分かれる，隔てる ②別れる，別れさせる 形 分かれた，別れた，別々の

□ **separator** 名 セパレーター，分離記号，分離子

□ **Seppo Linnainmaa** Seppo Linnainmaa《フィンランドの数学者およびコンピューター科学者》

□ **sequence** 名 ①連続（するもの），系列 ②列 ③順序，手順 ④結果

□ **sequential** 形 順次的な

□ **sequential data** 順次データ

□ **series** 名 一続き，連続，シリーズ

□ **serious** 形 ①まじめな，真剣な ②重大な，深刻な，（病気などが）重い

□ **serve** 動 ①仕える，奉仕する ②（役目を）果たす，務める，役に立つ

□ **service** 名 ①勤務，業務 ②公益事業 ③点検，修理 ④奉仕，貢献

□ **set up** 配置する，セットする，据え付ける，設置する

□ **setback** 名 ①後退，ぶり返し ②（建物の）セットバック，壁段後退

□ **severe** 形 厳しい，深刻な，激しい

□ **shape** 名 ①形，姿，型 ②状態，調子 動 形づくる，具体化する

□ **shocking** 形 衝撃的な，ショッキングな

□ **shortage** 名 不足，欠乏

□ **shortcoming** 名 欠点，短所，弱点

□ **should have done** ～すべきだった（のにしなかった）《仮定法》

□ **showbiz** 名 芸能界［産業］

□ **shown** 動 show（見せる）の過去分詞

□ **shut** 動 ①閉まる，閉める，閉じる ②たたむ ③閉じ込める ④shutの過去，過去分詞

□ **side** 名 側，横，そば，斜面 形 ①側面の，横の ②副次的な **side effect** 副作用，副次的影響

□ **signal** 名 信号，合図，信号機

□ **significant** 形 ①重要な，有意義な ②大幅な，著しい ③意味ありげな

□ **significantly** 副 著しく，かなり

□ **silence** 動 沈黙させる，静める

□ **silly** 形 おろかな，思慮のない

□ **similar** 形 同じような，類似した，相似の **be similar to** ～に似ている

□ **similarity** 名 類似（点），相似

□ **similarly** 副 同様に，類似して，同じように

□ **simply** 副 ①簡単に ②単に，ただ ③まったく，完全に

□ **simulate** 動 シミュレーションする，モデル化する

□ **single** 形 ①たった1つの ②1人用

の，それぞれの ③独身の ④片道の

□ **singularity** 名特異点 **technological singularity** 技術的特異点《AIなどの技術が，自ら人間より賢い知能を生み出す事が可能になる時点を指す言葉》

□ **Siri** 名Siri《Appleの各OSに搭載されているバーチャルアシスタント》

□ **situated** 形位置した，(ある境遇に)ある

□ **situation** 名①場所，位置 ②状況，境遇，立場

□ **sketch** 名スケッチ，草案

□ **skill** 名①技能，技術 ②上手，熟練

□ **skip** 動(途中を)抜かす，飛ばす

□ **slang** 名俗語，スラング

□ **slave** 名奴隷

□ **slight** 形①わずかな ②ほっそりして ③とるに足らない

□ **SLIP** 名SLIP《ワイゼンバウムが独自に開発したプログラミング言語》

□ **slow down** 速度を落とす

□ **slowly** 副遅く，ゆっくり

□ **smart** 形①利口な，抜け目のない ②きちんとした，洗練された

□ **smart wearable** スマートウェアラブル(デバイス)

□ **Smart Data Query (SDQ)** Smart Data Query《AIを用いたデータ出力要求。複雑で手間のかかる臨床データ解析を効率化させた》

□ **smartphone** 名スマートフォン

□ **smartwatch** 名スマートウオッチ

□ **smoothly** 副滑らかに，流ちょうに

□ **so as to** ～するように，～するために

□ **so far** 今までのところ，これまでは

□ **so that** ～するために，それで，～できるように

□ **so ~ that ...** 非常に～なので…

□ **so-called** 形いわゆる

□ **social** 形①社会の，社会的な ②社交的な，愛想のよい

□ **social media-based** ソーシャルメディアを基盤とした

□ **society** 名社会，世間

□ **Society of Automotive Engineers (SAE)** 米国自動車技術者協会《モビリティ専門家を会員とする米国の非営利団体》

□ **sociologist** 名社会学者

□ **software** 名ソフト(ウェア)

□ **Software Toolworks** ソフトウェア・ツールワークス《アメリカのソフトウェアおよびビデオゲーム開発会社》

□ **soil** 名土，土地

□ **soldier** 名兵士，兵卒

□ **solution** 名①分解，溶解 ②解決，解明，回答

□ **solve** 動解く，解決する

□ **someone** 代ある人，誰か

□ **something** 代①ある物，何か ②いくぶん，多少

□ **sometimes** 副時々，時たま

□ **sophisticated** 形①洗練された，都会的な ②世慣れた，上品ぶった

□ **sort** 名種類，品質 **a sort of** ～のようなもの，一種の～

□ **sound like** ～のように聞こえる

□ **South Korean** 形韓国の

□ **space station** 宇宙ステーション

□ **spam** 名スパム《受け手が望んでいない大量のメッセージを無差別に送ること》

□ **Spanish** 形スペイン(人・語)の 名①スペイン人 ②スペイン語

□ **specialized** 形専門の，分化した

□ **specific** 形明確な，はっきりした，具体的な

□ **specifically** 副特に，明確に，具体

的に

□ **speech recognition** 音声認識, 言語認識

□ **speed** 名速力, 速度 動①急ぐ, 急がせる ②制限速度以上で走る, スピード違反をする

□ **spell** 名①一続き, ひとしきり ②呪文, まじない

□ **spelling** 名つづり(方), スペル

□ **spin** 動①つむぐ ②(ガラス, 金などを)糸にする ③(カイコやクモが糸を)吐く ④ぐるぐる回る, スピンする 名①回転 ②(飛行機などの)きりもみ降下 ③《a－》急落

□ **spiritual** 形精神の, 精神的な, 霊的な

□ **split** 動裂く, 裂ける, 割る, 割れる, 分裂させる[する]

□ **spoil** 動①台なしにする, だめになる ②甘やかす

□ **spoiler** 名ネタバレ

□ **spoiler alert** ネタバレ注意

□ **spot** 動①～を見つける ②点を打つ, しみをつける

□ **spray** 動吹きかける

□ **squeak** 動①(ネズミなどが)チューチュー鳴く ②(楽器, 車輪などが)キーキーいう ③密告する 名①チューチューという鳴き声 ②キーキーという音

□ **St. Petersburg** サンクト・ペテルブルク《ロシア》

□ **stable** 形安定した, 堅固な, 分解しにくい

□ **Stable Diffusion** ステーブル・ディフュージョン《テキスト入力されたワードからAIが自動で画像を生成する, オープンソースの画像生成AIサービス》

□ **stack** 動積み重ねる

□ **stage** 動上演する

□ **stand** 熟 **not stand a chance** まるで歯が立たない

□ **standard** 名標準, 規格, 規準

□ **Stanford (University)** スタンフォード大学

□ **Star Wars** 「スター・ウォーズ」《1977年に公開された同名の映画から始まるアメリカのスペースオペラシリーズ》

□ **StarCraft II** スタークラフト2《ブリザード・エンターテイメントが開発したスタークラフトの後続作品であるリアルタイムストラテジー・コンピューターゲーム》

□ **starvation** 名飢餓, 餓死

□ **state** 名①あり様, 状態 ②国家, (アメリカなどの)州 ③階層, 地位 動(正式に～を)述べる, 言葉にする

□ **statement** 名声明, 述べること

□ **state-of-the-art** 形最新式の, 最新鋭の

□ **statistical** 形統計の, 統計に基づく

□ **statistical bias** 統計的偏り, biasやバイアスの同義語

□ **statistician** 名統計学者

□ **statistics** 名統計(学), 統計資料

□ **steadily** 副しっかりと

□ **steady** 形①しっかりした, 安定した, 落ち着いた ②堅実な, まじめな

□ **steering** 名(乗り物などの)かじ取り

□ **stereo** 名ステレオ

□ **stereo camera** ステレオカメラ《対象物を複数の異なる方向から同時に撮影することにより, その奥行き方向の情報も記録できるようにしたカメラ》

□ **stereotype** 名ステレオタイプ, 定型, 固定観念

□ **stock** 名①貯蔵 ②仕入れ品, 在庫品 ③株式

□ **Stockfish 8** Stockfish 8《Stockfishはフリーでオープンソースのチェスエンジン。2017年12月,

A B C D E F G H I J K L M N O P Q R S T U V W X Y Z

Stockfish 8はGoogle部門DeepMindのAlphaZeroをテストするベンチマークとして使用された》

□ **Stockholm** 名 ストックホルム

□ **stop doing** ～するのをやめる

□ **straightforward** 形 まっすぐな, 正直な, 率直な

□ **strategy** 名 戦略, 作戦, 方針

□ **streaming** 名 ストリーミング

□ **strength** 名 ①力, 体力 ②長所, 強み ③強度, 濃度

□ **stress** 名 ①圧力 ②ストレス ③強勢

□ **stride** 名 ①大またで歩くこと ②一またぎ

□ **strong AI** 強いAI《人類よりも優れた推論能力を持つAI(人工知能)のこと》

□ **strongly** 副 強く, 頑丈に, 猛烈に, 熱心に

□ **structural** 形 構造(上)の

□ **structure** 名 構造, 骨組み, 仕組み 動 (～を)構造化する, 構築する

□ **structured** 形 (物事が)計画[組織化・構造化]された

□ **struggle** 動 もがく, 奮闘する

□ **Stuart Russell** スチュアート・J・ラッセル《人工知能への貢献で知られる英国のコンピューター科学者》

□ **stuck** 動 stick(刺さる)の過去, 過去分詞

□ **studio** 名 ①スタジオ, 仕事場 ②ワンルームマンション

□ **style** 名 やり方, 流儀, 様式, スタイル

□ **submit** 動 ①服従する, 服従させる ②提出する

□ **sub-node** 名 サブノード, 子ノード《ルートノードでないノードのこと》

□ **subroutine** 名 サブルーチン

□ **subsequent** 形 次の, 続いて起きる, その結果生じた

□ **subset** 名 サブセット, (大集団の中の)小集団

□ **subsidiary** 名 ①子会社, 関連子会社 ②付属(物)

□ **substitution** 名 ①代用, 代理 ②入れ換え, 置換

□ **success** 名 成功, 幸運, 上首尾

□ **successful** 形 成功した, うまくいった

□ **successfully** 副 首尾よく, うまく

□ **successor** 名 後継者, 相続人, 後任者

□ **such as** たとえば～, ～のような

□ **such ~ as ...** …のような～

□ **sufficiently** 副 十分に, 足りて

□ **suggest** 動 ①提案する ②示唆する

□ **suggestion** 名 ①提案, 忠告 ②気配, 暗示

□ **suitable** 形 適当な, 似合う, ふさわしい

□ **sum** 動 ①合計する ②要約する

□ **summarize** 動 要約する

□ **super** 形 超一流の, 特大の

□ **supercomputer** 名 スーパーコンピューター

□ **superficial** 形 表面の, うわべだけの

□ **super-intelligent** 形 超知性的な

□ **supervise** 動 監督する

□ **supervised** 形 教師付きの

□ **supervised learning** 教師あり学習《学習データに正解を与えた状態で学習させる手法》

□ **support** 動 ①支える, 支持する ②養う, 援助する 名 ①支え, 支持 ②援助, 扶養

□ **support vector machine (SVM)** サポートベクターマシン

《機械学習モデルの一種で，教師あり学習を用いるパターン認識モデルの1つ。分類や回帰へ適用できる》

□ **support-vector** 名 サポートベクター《データを分割する直線に最も近いデータ》

□ **Support-vector networks** Support-vector networks《コリーナ・コルテスとウラジミール・ヴァプニク共著による1995年の論文》

□ **supposed** 形 想定されている **be supposed to** ～することになっている，～するはずである

□ **surely** 副 確かに，きっと

□ **surface** 名 ①表面，水面 ②うわべ，外見

□ **surpass** 動 勝る，しのぐ

□ **surprisingly** 副 驚くほど(に)，意外にも

□ **suspect** 名 容疑者，注意人物

□ **suspicion** 名 ①容疑，疑い ②感づくこと

□ **sustainability** 名 持続可能性

□ **SVM** 略 サポートベクターマシン《機械学習モデルの一種で，教師あり学習を用いるパターン認識モデルの1つ。分類や回帰へ適用できる。support vector machine の略》

□ **swarm** 名 群れ，群集，多数

□ **switch** 動 切り替える，切り替わる

□ **symbolic** 形 象徴する，象徴的な

□ **symbolic AI** シンボリックAI《1950年代に遡る，第1次AIブームで支配的だったパラダイムで，知識を記号で表現し，問題を解くために推論など，記号上の計算を行う》

□ **symphony** 名 ①交響楽，シンフォニー ②(音・色の)調和

□ **synthetic** 形 ①人工の ②合成の ③統合的な

□ **synthetic organic matter** 合成有機物

□ **system** 熟 **expert system** エキスパートシステム《人工知能研究から生まれたコンピューターシステムで，人間の専門家の意思決定能力をエミュレートするもの》

□ **systematic** 形 体系的な，計画的な

□ **systemic** 形 体系の，システムの

□ **systemic bias** 系統的バイアス《統計的な測定に，外部の圧力が影響を与えること》 **systemic racism** 制度的人種差別

T

□ **tactics** 名 戦術，戦法

□ **tactile** 形 触覚の

□ **tag** 名 札，値札

□ **take** 熟 **take advantage of** ～を利用する，～につけ込む **take away** ①連れ去る ②取り上げる，奪い去る ③取り除く **take care of** ～の世話をする，～の面倒を見る，～を管理する **take control of** ～を制御[管理]する，支配する **take over** 引き継ぐ，支配する，乗っ取る **take place** 行われる，起こる **take time to** ～するための時間を取る

□ **Talos** 名 タロース《ギリシア神話に登場する，クレータ島を守る自動人形(巨人)》

□ **target** 名 標的，目的物，対象

□ **task** 名 (やるべき)仕事，職務，課題

□ **tax** 名 ①税 ②重荷，重い負担

□ **Tay** 名 Tay《マイクロソフトによるおしゃべりボットで，Twitter上で書き込むボットとして2016年3月23日にお披露目された》

□ **technical** 形 技術(上)の，工業の，専門の

□ **technically** 副 技術的に，厳密には

□ **technique** 名 テクニック，技術，手法

□ **technological** 名技術上の，(科学)技術の

□ **technological singularity** 技術的特異点《AIなどの技術が，自ら人間より賢い知能を生み出す事が可能になる時点を指す言葉》

□ **technology** 名テクノロジー，科学技術

□ **teenage** 形ティーンエイジャーの，10代の

□ **telescope** 名望遠鏡

□ **television** 名テレビ

□ **tell of** 〜について話す［説明する］

□ **temperature** 名温度，体温

□ **temperature-humidity index** 不快指数

□ **tend** 動①(〜の)傾向がある，(〜)しがちである ②面倒を見る，手入れをする

□ **tendency** 名傾向，風潮，性癖

□ **Tenth Symphony** (ベートーヴェンの)第10交響曲

□ **term** 名①期間，期限 ②語，用語 ③《-s》条件 ④《-s》関係，仲

□ **terminate** 動終わらせる，終わる

□ **Terminator, The** 『ターミネーター』《アメリカのSFアクション映画，1984年》

□ **terms** 熟 **in terms of** 〜の言葉で言えば，〜の点から

□ **terribly** 副ひどく

□ **Tesla** テスラモーターズ《アメリカの電気自動車専業メーカー》

□ **Tesla Model S** テスラ・モデルS《アメリカのテスラ社が製造・販売している高級セダンタイプの電気自動車》

□ **Tesler's theorem** テスラーの定理《アメリカ合衆国のコンピューター科学者ラリー・テスラーがAI効果を定式化したもの。「知能とは，機械がまだやっていないことである」》

□ **test** 熟 **Turing test** チューリング・テスト《アラン・チューリングが提案した，ある機械が「人間的」かどうかを判定するためのテスト》

□ **test bed** テストベッド《新技術の実証試験に使用されるプラットフォーム》

□ **testing** 名テストすること

□ **text** 名本文，原本，テキスト，教科書 **predictive text** 入力予測《コンピューターで文字を入力する際，入力したい語をソフトウェアが予測・提示する機能》

□ **text-based** 形テキストベースの

□ **textbook** 名教科書

□ **textile** 形織物の

□ **thank ~ for** 〜に対して礼を言う

□ **thanks to** 〜のおかげで，〜の結果

□ **theater** 名劇場

□ **Théâtre D'opéra Spatial (Space Opera Theater)** 「スペースオペラ劇場」《AIが生成したアート。2022年，コロラド州の公共イベント「ステート・フェア」の美術作品コンテストのデジタルアート部門で最優秀賞に輝いた》

□ **theorem** 名定理《数学・論理学》

□ **theorist** 名理論家

□ **theory** 名理論，学説

□ **therapeutic** 形治療上の

□ **there** 熟 **here and there** あちこちで

□ **therefore** 副したがって，それゆえ，その結果

□ **thermostat** 名温度自動調節器，サーモスタット

□ **thesis** 名①(学位)論文 ②命題，テーマ，主張

□ **think of** 〜のことを考える，〜を思いつく，考え出す

□ **thinking** 名考えること，思考

□ **Thomas Paine** トマス・ペイン

A B C D E F G H I J K L M N O P Q R S T U V W X Y Z

《イギリス出身のアメリカ合衆国の哲学者, 政治活動家, 政治理論家, 革命思想家。1737–1809》

□ **though** 接 ①〜にもかかわらず, 〜だが ②たとえ〜でも **even though** 〜であるけれども, 〜にもかかわらず

□ **thousands of** 何千という

□ **threat** 名 おどし, 脅迫

□ **3x5** 3×5インチ

□ **360-degree** 形 360度の

□ **threshold** 名 ①敷居 ②出発点 ②閾(値) ④境界

□ **through** 熟 **pass through** 〜を通る, 通行する

□ **throughout** 前 ①〜中, 〜を通じて ②〜のいたるところに

□ **thumbnail** 名 親指の爪

□ **thus** 副 ①このように ②これだけ ③かくて, だから

□ **tic-tac-toe** 名 三目並べ《3×3の格子を用意し, 二人が交互に「○」と「×」を書き込んでいき3つ並べるゲーム。英国名はnoughts and crosses》

□ **time** 熟 **at a time** 一度に, 続けざまに **at the time** そのころ, 当時は **by the time** 〜する時までに **every time** 〜するときはいつも **for the first time** 初めて **in time** 間に合って, やがて **of the time** 当時の, 当節の **over time** 時間とともに, そのうち **take time to** 〜するための時間を取る

□ **timing** 名 適時選択, タイミング

□ **Tin Kam Ho** ティン・カム・ホウ《IBM Researchのコンピューター科学者》

□ **tiny** 形 ちっぽけな, とても小さい

□ **title** 名 ①題名, タイトル ②肩書, 称号 ③権利, 資格

□ **toaster** 名 トースター

□ **Tom Mustill** トム・マスティル《野生動物の映像作家》

□ **tone** 名 音, 音色, 調子

□ **tool** 名 道具, 用具, 工具

□ **Top Chess Engine Championship** Top Chess Engine Championship《2010年から開催されているコンピューター チェス トーナメント》

□ **topic** 名 話題, 見出し

□ **top-ranked** 形 一流の

□ **torso** 名 (人の)胴, トルソ《頭と手足のない人体像》

□ **total** 形 総計の, 全体の, 完全な 名 全体, 合計

□ **totally** 副 全体的に, すっかり

□ **tour** 名 ツアー, 見て回ること, 視察

□ **tournament** 名 トーナメント

□ **toxic** 形 中毒(性)の, 有毒な, 有害な

□ **track** 名 ①通った跡 ②競走路, 軌道, トラック **keep track of** 〜の経過を追う 動 追跡する

□ **tracker** 名 トラッカー《変動する情報を監視して, 最新情報を伝えるプログラム》

□ **tractor** 名 トラクター, 牽引するもの

□ **trade** 名 取引, 貿易, 商業 **make a trade** トレードする 動 取引する, 貿易する, 商売する

□ **trader** 名 ①商人, 貿易業者 ②投機家

□ **trading** 名 取引 **algorithmic trading** アルゴリズム取引《一度に処理しきれないほどの大口の注文を, プログラムによる自動取引により, 時間・価格・出来高に基づき, より小さな注文に分割して発注する取引方法の事。投資銀行や年金基金や投資信託会社やヘッジファンドで広く利用されている》

□ **traffic** 名 通行, 往来, 交通(量), 貿易

□ **tragedy** 名 悲劇, 惨劇

□ **trailer** 名（自動車にけん引される）トレーラー

□ **training** 名 ①トレーニング，訓練 ②コンディション，体調

□ **transaction** 名 ①取引 ②処理，取り扱い

□ **transfer** 動 ①移動する ②移す ③譲渡する

□ **transform** 動 ①変形［変化］する，変える ②変換する

□ **Transformer** 名 Transformer《Google Researchが生み出したニューラルネットワークアーキテクチャー》

□ **translate** 動 ①翻訳する，訳す ②変える，移す

□ **translation** 名 翻訳，言い換え，解釈

□ **transportation** 名 交通（機関），輸送手段

□ **trap** 動 わなを仕掛ける，わなで捕らえる

□ **traveling salesman problem (TSP)** 巡回セールスマン問題《セールスマンが所定の複数の都市を1回だけ巡回する場合の最短経路を求める組合せ最適化問題》

□ **treatment** 名 ①取り扱い，待遇 ②治療（法）

□ **tree** 熟 **decision tree** 決定木《木構造を用いて分類や回帰を行う機械学習の手法の一つ》 **regression tree** 回帰木《連続して変わりうる値を分析する場合に用いられる》 **search tree** 探索木《計算機科学において特定のキーを特定するために使用される木構造》

□ **trend** 名 トレンド，傾向

□ **trial** 名 ①試み，試験 ②苦難 ③裁判 形 試みの，試験の

□ **trick** 動 だます

□ **trillion** 名 1兆

□ **trilogy** 名 3部作

□ **trivia** 名 ①取るに足りないこと ②雑学的知識

□ **troll** 名〈軽蔑的〉嫌なやつ **Internet troll** インターネット・トロール《インターネット上での嫌がらせ行為。特に，ツイッターやフェースブックなどのソーシャルメディアで，悪意あるコメントをしつこく投稿したり，他人の話し合いを妨害したりすることを指す》

□ **trolley** 名 ①ワゴン，手押し車，台車 ②市街電車，トローリーバス

□ **trolley problem** トロッコ問題《「ある人を助けるために他の人を犠牲にするのは許されるか？」という形で功利主義と義務論の対立を扱った倫理学上の問題・課題》

□ **troublemaker** 名 ごたごたを起こす人

□ **truck** 名 トラック，運搬車

□ **truly** 副 ①全く，本当に，真に ②心から，誠実に

□ **trust** 動 信用［信頼］する，委託する 名 信用，信頼，委託

□ **TSP** 略 巡回セールスマン問題《セールスマンが所定の複数の都市を1回だけ巡回する場合の最短経路を求める組合せ最適化問題。traveling salesman problemの略》

□ **tube** 名 管，筒 **vacuum tube** 真空管

□ **tunnel** 名 トンネル

□ **Tuomas Sandholm** トゥオマス・サンドホルム《カーネギーメロン大学大学教授，連続起業家。2017年，学生のノーム・ブラウンと共に開発したＡＩ「リブラトゥス」がポーカーの一種「テキサス・ホールデム」の試合で4人のトッププレイヤーを相手に大勝を飾った》

□ **turban** 名 ターバン

□ **Turing test** チューリング・テスト《アラン・チューリングが提案した，ある機械が「人間的」かどうかを判定するためのテスト》

A B C D E F G H I J K L M N O P Q R S T U V W X Y Z

☐ **Turk,The** トルコ人《18世紀後半に作られた『チェス』を指すオートマタ(自動人形)。後に悪戯(中に人間が入って動作させていた)と判明》

☐ **Turkish** 形トルコ(人・語)の 名トルコ語

☐ **turn off** ①興味を失う, ～にうんざりする ②～を止める, (照明などを)消す ③(道から)それる, (道が)～から分かれる

☐ **turn out to be** ～という結果になる

☐ **turn to** ～の方を向く, ～に頼る, ～に変わる

☐ **turn-based** 形ターン制(の)

☐ **tweet** 動ツイートする 名ツイート

☐ **twitter** 名①さえずり, くすくす笑い ②《T-》ツイッター

☐ **two-dimensional** 形2次元の

☐ **typical** 形典型的な, 象徴的な

U

☐ **UBI** 略最低所得保障《universal basic incomeの略》

☐ **UC Berkeley** カリフォルニア大学バークレー校

☐ **UN Convention on Certain Conventional Weapons** 国際連合軍縮部

☐ **UN Security Council** 国連安全保障理事会

☐ **unable to** 《be –》～することができない

☐ **unavoidable** 形避けられない

☐ **unbelievable** 形信じられない(ほどの), 度のはずれた

☐ **uncanny** 形(気味が悪いほど)異様な

☐ **unconscious** 形無意識の, 気絶した

☐ **uncontrollable** 形制御できない

☐ **underestimated** 形少なく見積もって

☐ **underperform** 動(標準・平均よりも)低い働きをする

☐ **under-sampled** 形サンプル不足の

☐ **understandable** 形理解できる, わかる

☐ **understanding** 動understand(理解する)の現在分詞 名理解, 意見の一致, 了解 形理解のある, 思いやりのある

☐ **undoubtedly** 副疑う余地なく

☐ **unexpected** 形思いがけない, 予期しない

☐ **unexpressive** 形感情を殺した, ポーカーフェイスで

☐ **unfair** 形不公平な, 不当な

☐ **unfamiliar** 形よく知らない, なじみのない, 不案内な

☐ **unfold** 動展開する, ～を開く[広げる]

☐ **unforeseeable** 形予測[予見]不可能な

☐ **unfortunately** 副不幸にも, 運悪く

☐ **unhappy** 形不運な, 不幸な

☐ **unhelpful** 形助けにならない

☐ **unique** 形唯一の, ユニークな, 独自の

☐ **unit** 名ユニット, 構成単位, 1個, 1人

☐ **United States** 名アメリカ合衆国《国名》

☐ **universal** 形①全体の, 全世界の ②普遍的な

☐ **universal basic income (UBI)** 最低所得保障

☐ **universal language** 汎用言語

☐ **universe** 名《the – /the U-》宇宙, 全世界

□ **university** 名（総合）大学

□ **University of Alberta** アルバータ大学《カナダ》

□ **University of California, Berkeley** カリフォルニア大学バークレー校

□ **unknown** 形知られていない，不明の

□ **unlike** 前～と違って

□ **unlock** 動かぎを開ける，解く

□ **unopenable** 形開けられない

□ **unprecedented** 形前例［先例］のない

□ **unrelated** 形関係のない，親類でない

□ **unreliable** 形当てにならない，信頼できない

□ **unstable** 形不安定な，ぐらぐらする

□ **unstructured** 形非構造化の

□ **unsupervised** 形教師なしの

□ **unsupervised learning** 教師なし学習《あえて正解が決まっていないデータをコンピューターに与え，AIが自律的に答えを判断できるよう学習させる手法》

□ **untrue** 形真実でない，事実に反する

□ **unusual** 形普通でない，珍しい，見［聞き］慣れない

□ **unvisited** 形（場所などが）訪れる人のない

□ **unwelcome** 形歓迎されない，受け入れたくない

□ **up** 熟 **be made up of** ～で構成されている **come up with** ～に追いつく，～を思いつく，考え出す，見つけ出す **give up on** ～に見切りをつける **go up against**（対戦相手・上司など）に立ち向かう **look up** 調べる **make up** 作り出す，考え出す，～を構成［形成］する **open up** 広がる，広げる，開く，開ける **set up** 配置する，セットする，据え付ける，設置する

□ **update** 動最新にする，アップデートする

□ **upfront** 形前もっての，前払いの

□ **upfront cost** 初期費用

□ **upgrade** 動アップグレードする

□ **upheaval** 名（社会・経済・生活などの）大混乱

□ **upload** 名アップロード（すること）

□ **upon** 前 ①《場所・接触》～（の上）に ②《日・時》～に ③《関係・従事》～に関して，～について，～して

□ **uprising** 名 ①起床，起立 ②反乱，暴動，謀反

□ **upset** 形憤慨して，動揺して

□ **use** 熟 **make use of** ～を利用する，～を生かす

□ **used** 動 ①use（使う）の過去，過去分詞 ②《－to》よく～したものだ，以前は～であった 形 ①慣れている，《get［become］－to》～に慣れてくる ②使われた，中古の

□ **usefulness** 名役に立つこと，有用性

□ **user** 名使用者，利用者，消費者

□ **utilize** 動利用する，活用する

□ **utterly** 副まったく，完全に

V

□ **vaccine** 名ワクチン

□ **vacuum** 名真空，空白 **vacuum tube** 真空管

□ **validate** 動正当と認める，批准する

□ **value** 名価値，値打ち，価格 **discrete value** 離散値

□ **van** 名（小型）トラック，バン

□ **variable** 名 ①変わりやすいもの ②（数学で）変数

□ **variation** 名変化，変化に富むこと，

ばらつき

□ **variety** 名 ①変化, 多様性, 寄せ集め ②種類

□ **various** 形 変化に富んだ, さまざまの, たくさんの

□ **vary** 動 変わる, 変える, 変更する, 異なる

□ **vast** 形 広大な, 巨大な, ばく大な

□ **vector** 名 ①軌道, ベクトル, 衝動 ②媒介動物

□ **vehicle** 名 乗り物, 車, 車両

□ **version** 名 ①バージョン, 版, 翻訳 ②意見, 説明, 解釈

□ **vertex** 名 頂点

□ **vertical** 形 垂直の, 縦の

□ **vertical farm** 垂直農園

□ **vertical farming** 垂直農法《高層建築物の階層, 及び高層の傾斜面を使用して垂直的に農作業, 動物の育成を行う方法》

□ **vertices** 名 vertex (頂上, 最高点) の複数形

□ **victory** 名 勝利, 優勝

□ **viewer** 名 視聴者, 観察者

□ **viral** 形 (ソーシャルメディアを使って) 口コミで素早く広がる, バイラルの

□ **viral meme** バイラルミーム《インターネットを通じて人から人へと, 通常は模倣として, ウイルスの感染のように拡がっていく行動・コンセプト・メディアのこと》

□ **virtual** 形 ①事実上の ②仮想の

□ **virtual personal assistant** 仮想パーソナルアシスタント《個人のタスクまたはサービスを実行できるソフトウェアエージェント》

□ **virus** 名 ウイルス

□ **vision** 名 ①視力 ②先見, 洞察力

□ **visual** 形 視覚の, 視力の, 目に見える

□ **visual perception** 視覚

□ **Vladimir Vapnik** ウラジミール・ヴァプニク《サポートベクターマシンやサポートベクタークラスタリング, VC 理論の生みの親の一人で, 統計的学習の多くの基本的な概念を作り上げた》

□ **volume** 名 ①本, 巻, 冊 ②《-s》たくさん, 多量 ③量, 容積

□ **vote** 名 投票 (権), 票決

□ **voter** 名 投票者

□ **voting** 名 投票

□ **vowel** 名 母音 (字)

W

□ **wager** 動 賭ける

□ **walk around** 歩き回る, ぶらぶら歩く

□ **Walter Pitts** ウォルター・ピッツ《アメリカ合衆国の論理学者・数学者。1943年, 神経生理学者・外科医のウォーレン・マカロックと共に, 形式ニューロンというモデルを考えた。1923-1969》

□ **Walter Werzowa** ウォルター・ワーゾワ《オーストリアの作曲家, プロデューサー》

□ **warfare** 名 戦争, 交戦状態, 戦闘行為

□ **warn** 動 警告する, 用心させる

□ **warning** 名 警告, 警報

□ **Warren McCulloch** ウォーレン・マカロック《アメリカ合衆国の神経生理学者で外科医。1943年, 論理学者・数学者のウォルター・ピッツと共に, 形式ニューロンというモデルを考えた。1898-1969》

□ **Watson** 名 ワトソン《IBMが開発した質問応答システム・意思決定支援システム。IBMはワトソンを「Augmented Intelligence, 拡張知能」, 自然言語を理解・学習し人間の意思決定を支援する『コグニティブ・コン

ピューティング・システム（Cognitive Computing System）』と定義している》

□ **Watson Discovery** Watson Discovery《HTML, PDFといった形式で作成された文書をIBMの人工知能「Watson」によって，コンテンツを検索するシステム》

□ **wave** 名 ①波 ②（手などを）振ること

□ **way** 熟 **all the way** ずっと **in a way** ある意味では **lead the way** 先に立って導く，案内する，率先する **long way** はるかに **way of** ～する方法

□ **weak AI** 弱いAI《人間の知能の一部に特化した機能を実現するAIのこと。特化型AIも似たような意味で使われる。narrow AIと同義》

□ **weakness** 名 ①弱さ，もろさ ②欠点，弱点

□ **wealth** 名 ①富，財産 ②豊富，多量

□ **weapon** 名 武器，兵器

□ **weaponized** 形 兵器化した

□ **wearable** 形 身に着けられる，ウェアラブルな **smart wearable** スマートウェアラブル（デバイス）

□ **weave** 動 織る，編む

□ **weaver** 名 織り手

□ **web** 名 ①クモの巣 ②《the W-》ウェブ（=World Wide Web）

□ **webcam** 名 ウェブカメラ

□ **website** 名 ウェブサイト

□ **weight** 名 ①重さ，重力，体重 ②重荷，負担 ③重大さ，勢力

□ **well** 熟 **as well** なお，その上，同様に **as well as** ～と同様に

□ **well-defined** 形 明確に定義された

□ **well-known** 形 よく知られた，有名な

□ **well-suited** 形（目的を達成するのに）適切な，適合した

□ **whale** 名 クジラ（鯨）

□ **what if** もし～だったらどうなるだろうか

□ **whatever** 代 ①《関係代名詞》～するものは何でも ②どんなこと[もの]が～とも 形 ①どんな～でも ②《否定文・疑問文で》少しの～も，何らかの

□ **wheel** 名 ①輪，車輪，《the –》ハンドル ②旋回

□ **when it comes to** ～に関して言えば

□ **whenever** 接 ①～するときはいつでも，～するたびに ②いつ～しても

□ **whereby** 副 ①～するところの，それによって ②どういう手段で，何について

□ **wherein** 副 そこで，その場所で

□ **whether** 接 ～かどうか，～かまたは…，～であろうとなかろうと

□ **which** 熟 **of which** ～の中で

□ **while** 熟 **for a while** しばらくの間，少しの間

□ **whole** 形 全体の，すべての，完全な，満～，丸～ 名《the –》全体，全部 **as a whole** 全体として

□ **whom** 代 ①誰を[に] ②《関係代名詞》～するところの人，そしてその人を

□ **wide** 形 幅の広い，広範囲の，幅が～ある

□ **widely** 副 広く，広範囲にわたって

□ **will have done** ～してしまっているだろう《未来完了形》

□ **winner** 名 勝利者，成功者

□ **winter** 熟 **AI winter** AIの冬，AI冬の時代

□ **wise** 形 賢明な，聡明な，博学の

□ **with** 熟 **agree with**（人）に同意する **along with** ～と一緒に **be familiar with** ～をよく知っている，～と親しい **be filled with** ～でいっ

ぱいになる **begin with** ～で始まる **come up with** ～に追いつく，～を思いつく，考え出す，見つけ出す **help out with** ～を手伝う

□ **within** 前 ①～の中［内］に，～の内部に ②～以内で，～を越えないで 名 内部

□ **witness** 動 ①目撃する ②証言する

□ **Wolfgang von Kempelen** ヴォルフガング・フォン・ケンペレン《ハンガリーの著述家ならびに発明家》

□ **wonder** 動 ①不思議に思う，（～に）驚く ②（～かしらと）思う **wonder if** ～ではないかと思う

□ **word** 熟 **in other words** すなわち，言い換えれば

□ **work** 熟 **at work** 働いて，仕事中で，（機械が）稼動中で **work in** ～の分野で働く，～に入り込む **work of** ～の仕業 **work on** ～で働く，～に取り組む，～を説得する，～に効く **work out** うまくいく，何とかなる，（問題を）解く，考え出す，答えが出る，～の結果になる

□ **world** 熟 **all over the world** 世界中に

□ **World Computer Chess Championship** 世界コンピューターチェス選手権《1974年から定期的に開催されている，コンピューター チェス エンジン同士が競い合うイベント》

□ **worried** 形 心配そうな，不安げな

□ **worse** 形 いっそう悪い，より劣った，よりひどい

□ **worth** 形（～の）価値がある，（～）しがいがある

□ **woven** 動 weave（織る）の過去分詞

□ **wrist** 名 手首，リスト

□ **writer** 名 書き手，作家

□ **writing** 名 ①書くこと，作文，著述 ②筆跡 ③書き物，書かれたもの，文書

□ **wrong** 熟 **go wrong** 失敗する，道を踏みはずす，調子が悪くなる

X

□ **XCON** 名 XCON《DECで開発された計算機システムのハードウェア，ソフトウェアの構成を決定するエキスパートシステムで，最初はR1と呼ばれていた》

□ **X-ray** 名 ①《しばしば-s》X線，レントゲン ②レントゲン写真［検査］

Y

□ **year** 熟 **for ～ years** ～年間，～年にわたって

□ **yet** 熟 **not yet** まだ～してない **yet another** さらにもう一つの **yet to** いまだ～されない

□ **Yoda-like** 形 ヨーダに似た《「ヨーダ」は『スター・ウォーズ』に登場する，ジェダイのマスター》

□ **YouTube** 名 ユーチューブ

□ **YouTuber** 名 YouTubeに動画を投稿する人

Z

□ **zero** 名 ゼロ，零，どん底，最低点 形 ゼロ［零］の

□ **zero-sum** 名 ゼロ・サム，ゼロ和

□ **zero-sum game** ゼロサムゲーム《参加者全員の負け分，勝ち分の総和がゼロになるゲーム。チェスや囲碁など》

ラダーシリーズ

Introduction to AI: Theory and Applications AIの未来

2023年3月1日 第1刷発行
2024年4月6日 第3刷発行

著　者　アンドリュー・ロビンス

発行者　浦　晋亮

発行所　IBCパブリッシング株式会社
〒162-0804 東京都新宿区中里町29番3号
菱秀神楽坂ビル
Tel. 03-3513-4511　Fax. 03-3513-4512
www.ibcpub.co.jp

印　刷　株式会社シナノパブリッシングプレス
装　丁　伊藤 理恵

Printed in Japan
ISBN978-4-7946-0747-8